the Church
the Body of Christ

the
Church
the Body of
Christ

**John
Mac Arthur, Jr.**

**ZONDERVAN
PUBLISHING HOUSE**
OF THE ZONDERVAN CORPORATION
GRAND RAPIDS, MICHIGAN 49506

To my beloved, Patricia,
who ministers to me most.

Acknowledgments

The material in this book began, for the most part, as a sermon series which formed the basis for the ministry of a growing, aggressive local congregation, Grace Community Church of Panorama City, California. I am deeply grateful for the congregation's willingness to be the crucible in which these truths are being tested. Thanks to them, this is not just theory; it is working. I am no expert, biblically or experimentally, but there is in my heart deep love for the truths presented here because they have made up the days and nights of my life for the past two years. I owe much to Jim Reapsome for adding his editorial ability so that these truths might be shared with others. The material is not original—many thoughts and terms are borrowed from other Spirit-taught men —and all that is mine is really the Spirit's, who has taught me during the hours in my study and living with my flock. Even my prayer is borrowed: "These things write I unto you, that your joy may be full."

Contents

Illustrations

Introduction

She went to London to die. Her husband was gone. The courts had decided she was an unfit mother and had given him the three children. Drugs, swinging parties, prostitution, perversion, money, jet-setting, excommunication from the Mormon church, and two abortions later, she landed in England. At the American Express window she met Jenny, one of the Manson family girls, the one who had smuggled dope into the Los Angeles jail for Charlie Manson, kept all the clan weapons, and did Sunset Boulevard vigils. All the newspapers had written about her. But Jenny was different—Jesus Christ had seen to that. She knew she could help. Francis A. Schaeffer was in London and the two girls finally found him. That was the beginning of the beginning. Sally met Jesus Christ!

Tom was crazed, incensed, frustrated. His wife had been unfaithful, and he was after the man. With the gun in hand for two days, he chased his victim, sandwiched between the pursuing police. His wife was in my office asking me to pray. In panicky frustration, he finally came home, fell on the floor—and for three hours wrestled with his anguish until he finally cried out to God. Liberty came, and peace. Tom received the Savior!

They weren't a family. They were three sick, sepa-

9

rated, and broken lives who happened to have the same last name and eat at the same table—sometimes. They were simple, middle-class people. The boys were drug addicts, Dad was a drunk. Nobody cared. Then a kid on the corner told them the good news of salvation. The Heaths are a family now, in Christ.

Phil was different, very different. He had all the best—the right family, the right money, the right girl, the right education (Harvard Law School), corporation lawyer and not yet thirty, the offer of a lifetime —the big money, the whole American dream. And in it all, Jesus Christ was first.

An embalmer by profession, Dave was a guy who looked as if he missed it all. Lonely, no family, no meaning. At twenty-one he sat in his car, put a gun to his head, and pumped in three bullets. Blood was everywhere, but not death. In semi-conscious thought, Jesus came back to him and Dave yielded. Two bullets are still there, and a large hole in his skull. It all affected his brain, his coordination, and his eternal soul.

Each of these stories is a biography by a divine Author. I know them all, teach them every week, and pray for and with them. They are part of my living every day. These persons had nothing, humanly, to bind them together—no common interests —until Jesus Christ made them one fellowship.

Sally found her way from London to L'Abri Fellowship in Switzerland. There she met Jeff, a young man with whom I had shared some of my life and teaching. He told her of our ministry and the fact that she could find a growing experience in this fellowship. Several months later she began the long trip here. At the London airport she discovered she had miscalculated and was short about $10 for her ticket to Los Angeles. She met Jeff, again, who had just found the amount she needed—it was lying on the ground. Together they flew here. We met one Sunday soon after that, and she became one of us. She is involved now, ministering her gifts to children as well as helping young people solve their problems.

Tom came to church the Sunday after his dramatic chase; his wife brought him. We met and he began to come regularly to Bible study. He devoured the Word like a starving man and grew so rapidly that in a few months he was building up his own library of Bible study tools and using them. Then came the desire to teach and the verification by the Body that he had the gift of teaching. A Sunday school class of 70 adults was next, then home Bible studies and prayer groups. God gave him great care for missions, and that became his concern and a service. All this in less than two years.

The Heaths were reached by a young man from our fellowship who shared Christ with one son. He came, grew in Christ, and reached his brother. Their lives began to speak to their dad; he came to see me, responded to Christ, and became part of the miracle on the block—a miracle that has touched more than twenty people. Immediately they began to participate in the fellowship, to be taught and ministered to by the Body. Now they are all involved in bringing drug addicts to Christ.

Phil came to us because he heard we taught the Word. He became involved in ministering his gifts among the newly married and soon was leading the fastest-growing part of our fellowship. Door-to-door evangelism teams and prayer groups function weekly under his leadership. He was offered the opportunity to take a position involving a great deal of money, with one of the world's largest corporations. I'll never forget seeing a copy of the letter he sent them; it said, in effect, that he could not accept their kind and generous offer because he felt committed to the Lord's work in his Bible class. I can imagine their shock!

Dave came because someone told him he could find fellowship and love here. He gave as much as he found. He began by being available to drive his car for junior high outings; then he entered all their activities and soon started to study the Word faithfully, equipping himself for teaching them. He received a group of boys. He taught them, chauffered them, heard their problems, and loved them; and it was mutual. We talked a lot about missions, and prayed. After a while the circumstances matched his heart's desire, and he began his training for service in another land as God directs. He is studying with a worldwide mission organization.

Frequently, all of them meet for prayer—to pray for each other and for all the saints and those to whom they take Christ. They are one—and they are only samples of a community of hippies, housewives, low-riders, lawyers, teachers, students, surfers, musicians, doctors, businessmen, factory workers—all sharing love and care for each other and reaching the world for Jesus Christ. Outside of Him, they have nothing in common; in Him, they are one, in every way.

This is the Body—the church. The blueprint for it is the theme of this book.

the Church
the Body of Christ

JOHN 10:1-15, 26-30

JOHN 15:1-10

COL. 1:13; ROM. 14:17

I COR. 12:1-27

EPH. 5:22-32

EPH. 2:19

CHRIST
EPH. 2:20-22

There are various metaphors for the church.

14

Chapter One

THE CHURCH: ONE BODY

What is the church? That is the question, and the answers are legion. Churches vary from well-structured, wealthy, highly organized institutions to underground cell groups with no money or structure, and everything in between.

What is the church? What is its biblical pattern and purpose? How do we express its identity and fulfill Christ's desire in creating it?

To begin, there are biblical metaphors which show what the church is—a family, a bride, a vineyard, a temple, a building, a kingdom, a flock, but most directly and specifically, a body.

The church is the body of Christ. All the other metaphors have Old Testament equivalents, but this one does not. The concept does not even exist in the Old Testament. The body is the church's New Testament identity, its unique position in Christ.

The church is not physical building, but a group of believers, not a denomination, sect, or association, but a spiritual body. The church is not an organization, but a *koinonia*—a communion, a fellowship—of one body, and it includes all believers. This unique metaphor forms the basis of our study.

Undergirding the scriptural teaching about the body of Christ is the concept of *unity*. I Corinthians 12:12 says:

> For as the body is one [here Paul talks about the physical body] and hath many members, and all the members of that one body, being many, are one body: so also is Christ.

Paul refers to the physical body and says, in effect, "You know that a physical being must be one. You cannot take a body and put an arm, a leg, head, heart, and a couple of feet together in a heap and tell the body to go do something. You cannot say to those disconnected members, 'Pull yourselves together and function.'"

A body is a unit of members functioning together, or it does not exist. I cannot say my hand is so gifted I will cut it off and send it alone to do a job. The hand would no longer be gifted; if I cut it off, it dies. Thus the essence of the body is unity. We are one, so also is Christ.

In the body, Christ is the head, and the head is the life. Looking at the metaphor from a different perspective, you can cut off a hand or an arm, but the head will maintain life. If you cut off the head, the life is gone, and the same thing is true in Christ's body. In Ephesians 5:23, Paul says, "Christ is the head of the church." That sounds like a simple thought, perhaps, but some people think they are the head of their churches. All believers are one in Him, receiving all resources, all strength, all wisdom, and all instructions from the same head.

I Corinthians 12:13 tells how a person enters the body of Christ:

> For by one Spirit are we all baptized into one body, whether we be Jews or Gentiles, whether we be bond or free; and have been all made to drink into one Spirit.

In verses 12 and 13 Paul refers to "one body" four times to emphasize body unity. Christians are one, and salvation is the initial point of their unity. Every Christian comes to God through Jesus Christ. They are united because they are all baptized by one Spirit into one body.

People often ask what the baptism of the Holy Spirit is. It is clearly this: God's Spirit placing a believer into the body of Christ. Verse 13 says exactly that: "By one Spirit are we *all* baptized into one body" (italics added). A Christian comes into the body of Christ at the moment of his salvation, being placed there by the energy of the Spirit. From the moment he received Jesus Christ he was a part of Christ's body. Not only was he put there but, verse 13 says, every Christian also has the same indwelling Spirit. "To drink" is to assimilate or appropriate the one Spirit.

So the Spirit regenerates all believers, places them in the body of Christ, and comes to indwell them. Every Christian? Yes. Romans 8:9 says, "If any man have not the Spirit of Christ, he is none of his." There is no such thing as a believer who doesn't have the Holy Spirit. Notice how the unity of the church is all wrapped up in the Spirit. Paul may say, in Ephesians 4:3, "Endeavouring to keep the unity of the Spirit in the bond of peace," because the same Spirit regenerates Christians, baptizes them into the body, and indwells them.

The church's unity, then, is not based upon an artificial, organizational relationship. Nor upon the fact that people are church-goers. Its basis is that all believers have been identified in the work of a single Spirit. He is the same in me as in any other Christian. I came to Jesus Christ and believed in him. I was regenerated by the Spirit in the same way, placed in the same body by the same Spirit in the same way, and indwelt by the same Spirit in the same way that all other Christians have been. Therefore, we are one *in the Spirit.*

Given that all Christians have received this unity and are one in the body of Christ, still they have a tendency to pull apart and to isolate themselves in smaller groups. They scatter into cliques, joining themselves to little groups of people who act and think the same way. It's possible for Christians to go to the same church meetings, sit together, and even talk superficially, but at heart still be far away from each other. They are tightly closed to most fellow believers, even though they may be open to a few. They have not learned to care and to express oneness in practical ways. They operate contrary to the way the body is supposed to function, and therefore the whole body is hindered. Much of our ministry involves getting people who are theoretically one to relate to each other, or, to put it another way, getting the members back together into the experience of the whole body as God intended.

"Super saints" do not exist. One minister said, "The church is so cold and the body so dead, that when someone arrives with a 98.6 temperature, we think he's sick. We think he has a fever, when actually he is normal." To be totally committed to Jesus Christ and totally absorbed in the Spirit's ministry is not to be "super"; it's to be normal. There are no great members in the body. No one can come in and say, "Well, how did you get here? I did this thing and forty-nine of those and seventy-four of those, and I got here." No, he didn't. He came by one Spirit into one body, just as everyone else did. That's the point of Christian unity. If works got us into the body, we would all burst with pride. Instead, we are trophies of grace, brought into the body through Christ. Christians have nothing personal to boast about.

The clergy-laity dichotomy is, in that context at least, unbiblical. As a preacher, I am no higher than a layman, except that my pulpit is raised thirty-six inches. I am not above another believer, and he is not above anyone else; neither is he below anyone. No hierarchy is expressed in the body metaphor. There are varying gifts, which we will study later, but no hierarchy. The organizational chart of Christianity is simple—Christ the head, and then a body. There are levels of command and authority (I Tim. 5:17), but that is not to be equated with spiritual superiority. Leaders are not some kind of upper division Christians.

Every biblical metaphor of the church, without exception, emphasizes its unity. The church is one bride with one husband; one flock with one shepherd; one set of branches on one vine; one kingdom with one king; one family with one father; one building with one foundation; one body with one head, Jesus Christ. There is no room for hierarchy, no room for believers to feel like either upper- or lower-class Christians. Jesus did not say there are long and short branches; He did not say there are blue-ribbon sheep and also-rans. *Positionally*, each believer stands on the same ground in Christ.

There also is no such thing as an isolated believer— a believer by himself who is not part of the body. Whether babies, young men, or fathers spiritually (I John 2:12-14), Christians are one together; whether carnal or spiritual, they are one.

The Apostle Paul had to work with a church at Corinth that was badly split (I Cor. 1:12). Some Christians said, "I am an Apollos man myself." Others: "Well, not me, I'm a Paul man." "You're both wrong— Cephas is in," some said. Then the pious ones spoke, "Listen, folks, I follow Christ." Paul replied to this feeling in verse 13—"Is Christ divided?" and in 3:21— "Therefore let no man glory in men." Christians cannot say, "I follow him, or I follow that one." The apostle adds:

For all things are yours; Whether Paul, or Apollos, or Cephas, or the world, or life, or death, or things

19

present, or things to come; all are yours; And ye are Christ's; and Christ's is God's (I Cor. 3:21-23).

Christians are to end their party bickering and return to oneness. The church is one body—redeemed people who owe their distinct existence, their life together, to the fact that they were put into one body by one Spirit and indwelt by the same Spirit.

The New Testament word for church is *ekklesia,* which means "assembly" and is from a verb meaning "to call out." Christians are called apart from the world to assemble and exist as a separate entity. They are to lead a life worthy of His calling (Eph. 4:1), so that they become in character and conduct what they are by virtue of their union with Christ. The Christian life is the process of working out in practical matters the spiritual resources of the believer's position in Christ. The church is the company of God's people, called out of the world and separated to live for Him.

> That at that time ye were without Christ, being aliens from the commonwealth of Israel, and strangers from the covenants of promise, having no hope, and without God in the world: But now in Christ Jesus ye who sometimes were far off are made nigh by the blood of Christ. For he is our peace, who hath made both one [that is, Jew and Gentile], and hath broken down the middle wall of partition between us; Having abolished in his flesh the enmity . . . to make in himself of twain one new man, so making peace; And that he might reconcile both unto God in one body by the cross. . . . For through him we both have access by one Spirit unto the Father (Eph. 2:12-16, 18).

In the church,

> There is neither Jew nor Greek, there is neither bond nor free, there is neither male nor female, for ye are all one in Christ Jesus (Gal. 3:28).

Concerning the Christian's position in the blessings of Christ, none of these distinctions exists in the church. The church is "one new man" in Christ, a new body, a brand new thing; it never existed before. Christ has abolished the barriers of nationality, race, class, and sex to make all believers one, to make one new man.

Some people in the local church, however, have a hard time accepting this fact and allowing it to control their lives. They don't realize that in Christ all discrimination ends. The church that Christ has created, that He is head of, tolerates no distinctions.

During a special evangelistic effort among blacks of one community, our team was constantly under police surveillance. At one point we were arrested and fined, accused of stirring up the blacks. Then we were threatened with a public beating if we didn't stop our meetings. The chief of police was especially profane and abusive. I told him we were there only to preach Jesus Christ and asked him if he objected to that; he said he didn't and added that he himself was a Sunday school superintendent. We were released but constantly watched until the mission was over. (I learned later that the pastor of the police chief's church had had a nervous breakdown and finally took his own life, because of pressure from his own people when he began to extend concern and fellowship to blacks.)

In Romans 10:12, 13, Paul again states the message of church unity:

For there is no difference between the Jew and the Greek: for the same Lord over all is rich unto all that call upon him. For whosoever shall call upon the name of the Lord shall be saved.

All the barriers are gone, there are none left in Jesus Christ, the church is one new man.

Attaining unity was especially difficult in the early church because of the separation between Jews and Gentiles. However, Paul spoke directly to this problem:

Having abolished in his flesh the enmity, even the

law of commandments contained in ordinances; for to make in himself of twain one new man, so making peace (Eph. 2:15).

Jesus ended legalism as a principle of religion. He abolished "the enmity," the opposition between Jew and Gentile created by the law. The Jew was intent on keeping the law, and he glorified himself for doing so; at the same time, he looked down on those who didn't. The Gentile was outcast. But when Jesus died on the cross, He did away with external law-keeping as a testimony to faith. Therefore, the Gentile need no longer be kept out; he could move into the fullness of all God's blessings. There were no restrictions.

Scripture says the law was good in that it revealed God's holiness and man's sinfulness. When Jesus died, He fully accepted the punishment due sinners for law-breaking, but at the same time He met all the law's demands. The law, therefore, could make no more claims on Jew or Gentile. And if the law no longer keeps men from God, it doesn't separate men from each other. If Jew and Gentile were to be brought together, the enmity, the barrier, had to be abolished. That's what happened when Jesus died and rose from the dead.

In place of the old animosity Christ created "one new man." The barriers that separate men are down. In France during World War II, some GIs took the body of a buddy to a local cemetery. However, they were stopped by a priest, who said, "Sorry, boys, you can't bury your friend here if he's not a Catholic." Although discouraged, the GIs didn't give up; they decided to give burial just outside the cemetery fence. Next morning when they went to pay their last respects at the grave, they couldn't find it. After looking for an hour, they asked the priest about it. He explained: "Well, the first part of the night I stayed awake, sorry for what I had told you. The second part of the night I spent moving the fence."

So Jesus, in effect, moved the fence and included

every believer in God's promises, which are received by faith apart from the works of the law. He opened a common ground for all people to come to a knowledge of God. This means there is no reason for Christians not to love each other. Christ has removed human distinctions. In the "one new man" there is a new quality of existence; there has never been anything like the body of Christ.

Paul in his writings calls Christians four things: fellow heirs, fellow members, fellow partakers, fellow citizens. All these terms emphasize the unity of the body. Christians, therefore, are not to cut themselves off from fellow believers. Rather, their responsibility is to move into the mainstream of the life of the body. Some Christians, when they go to church, just sit as if to say, "Well, God, I know you're really blessed by my being here." They don't know what it means to live in the vitality and nourishment received from Christ's body. In effect, although sharing the same identity by virtue of their faith, they do not share the same practice. They weaken the outworking of the resources of Christ's body. Their failure to grow in their commitment affects everyone, because other believers try to compensate for their isolation and separateness.

Jesus wanted all believers to experience unity. So desperately did He want it that He prayed to His Father:

> Neither pray I for these alone [the disciples], but for them also which shall believe on me through their word; That they all may be one; as thou, Father, art in me, and I in thee, that they also may be one in us: that the world may believe that thou hast sent me (John 17:20, 21).

What will convince the world who Jesus is? Christian unity—we must be super-sensitive to one another. Verse 22:

> And the glory which thou gavest me I have given them; that they may be one, even as we are one.

23

Jesus put his glory in Christians, that they might be one, and his glory is the Holy Spirit (I Pet. 4:14). The presence of the Holy Spirit is the believer's point of unity. Verse 23:

> I in them, and thou in me, that they may be made perfect in one; and that the world may know that thou hast sent me, and hast loved them, as thou hast loved me.

When are Christians going to turn this world upside down? When are they going to shatter the complacency of this world? When they experience oneness! If a local congregation becomes one in body energy and begins to minister to the needs of each Christian with super-sensitive unity, the world will never be able to cope with the results; that local church will release the unity and the energy of the Holy Spirit.

How does Christian oneness work? I will show you two keys—*humility* and *love*. Jesus prayed that Christians would be one. Paul desired the same thing, but evidently the Christians at Philippi hadn't found it. In Philippians 2:2 Paul says, "Fulfill ye my joy, that ye be likeminded, having the same love, being of one accord, of one mind." What "mind" is that? Verse 5: "Let this mind be in you, which was also in Christ Jesus." Christians are to have the mind of Christ. What is the mind of Christ? Verses 6-8:

> Who, being in the form of God, thought it not robbery to be equal with God: But made himself of no reputation, and took upon him the form of a servant, and was made in the likeness of men: And being found in fashion as a man, he humbled himself, and became obedient unto death, even the death of the cross.

The mind of Christ is humility.

How do Christians experience unity? Verse 4:

> Look not every man on his own things, but every man also on the things of others.

Christians must be like Jesus and say, "I don't care about me, all I care about is you." Can you imagine what would happen if all Christians went around caring nothing for themselves and caring everything for everyone else? Each Christian would get the care he needs. Each one would have the whole body caring for him. Many Christians spend so much time on themselves that no one can tolerate caring for them. If Christians ever learn—and by God's Spirit they may—to start caring for each other, they will be drowned in care and love. That is the mind of humility. No wounded egos, no stepped-on toes, no "I'm not speaking to Mrs. So-and-so anymore," no "That is the last time I'll do that." That is not humility, but ego, plain ego.

Christ never tried to maintain His ego when He came here. They spat on Him, and He just stood there. They nailed Him to a cross, and He just hanged there. He didn't say, "You can't do this to me, I won't tolerate it." The mind of humility says, "If this means your salvation and your benefit and blessing, I'll suffer because I care about you." That is something of a foreign idea to contemporary Christian experience, but it's what the body concept is all about. Selfless Paul had this in mind: "If I be offered upon the sacrifice and service of your faith, I joy" (Phil. 2:17). He was expendable for the sake of others.

In Romans 12:3, 4 Paul says, "For I say, through the grace given unto me, to every man that is among you, not to think of himself more highly than he ought to think; ... For as we have many members in one body ..." Christians are all in Christ's body. They experience unity by thinking about others instead of themselves. Christians need not worry about their egos; they need not worry about their little thoughts. They can start by reaching out and touching someone else's life. Christians are one, and the point of contact for their unity must be humility.

How far does humility go? A Christian could get trampled. So get trampled! God can restore you. Paul condemns a Christian who sues another Christian, goes to court, and hassles publicly with him.

> Now therefore there is utterly a fault among you, because ye go to law one with another. Why do ye not rather take wrong?

Just take it. A person might say, "But you don't know how much it was." Take it!

> Why do ye not rather suffer yourselves to be defrauded? Nay, ye do wrong, and defraud, and that your brethren (I Cor. 6:7, 8).

Take it, just take it. Paul says Christians are to care so much for each other that they can care less what happens to them. Some brother may defraud a believer, but some other brother is going to pick him up, because a giving and loving person receives what he gives and gets back the love he gives away. Paul adds, in effect, that if he dies in ministering to others, that is only "gain" (cf. Phil. 1:12-21). Each of us is expendable for each other.

Humility is the first key to experiencing Christian oneness. The second key, which overlaps humility, is love. Jesus says, "A new commandment I give unto you, That ye love one another" (John 13:34). This love doesn't care what happens; it is uncircumstantial. Love affects anyone—it doesn't matter what he does. Unlike human love, which is selective and based on attractiveness, this love doesn't pick and choose. It is just there.

Sometimes one believer will say of another, "I love her in the Lord." This is a lot like saying, "I hate her." It is as if a Christian had a little valve and squirted the other one with eight drops of divine love, unmixed with his own, and then shut it off. But, in truth, either we love another or we don't. Jesus said love is not an option, but a new commandment. Christians don't have a natural capacity to love everyone, but "the love of God is shed abroad in our hearts" (Rom. 5:5).

How are Christians to love?

As I have loved you, that ye also love one another. By this shall all men know that ye are my disciples, if ye have love one to another (John 13:34, 35).

Christians may convince the world that Jesus is for real by loving one another. The greatest evangelism in the world is not having a big revival; it is having so much love that the world can't figure it out. The mark of Christian unity is love. "The Lord make you to increase and abound in love one toward another," Paul prayed (I Thess. 3:12). John said, "This is the message that ye heard from the beginning, that we should love one another" (I John 3:11).

Do Christians really love as Christ loved? Or are they so protective of their egos that every time something goes wrong they retaliate and get bitter? What do Christians do when everything isn't the way they think it should be, if Sister So-and-so and Brother So-and-so irritate them? Then are they angry and bitter? Or are they kind and loving, not caring about the circumstances? Does their love just pour out, touching whoever is out there?

The love of Christian unity causes one believer to go to his brother and say, "Brother, I have had a bitterness against you, and I want to ask you to forgive me. I want to begin to love you." The love of church unity also says, "Brother, I forgive you." It says, "I'm sorry, brother." It doesn't criticize others to build up oneself. It loves no matter what the cost—money, prestige, position. If a person has anything but love for any fellow believer, he must pray to God, repent and confess, and then go to that believer and make it right, before the body of Christ will be healthy.

Again in I Corinthians 12, we note that the church

is not only unified but diversified—Christians are one and yet they are many. Verse 14:

For the body is not one member, but many.

The body is one, and yet there are arms, and fingers, and all the various parts and organs of the body, each with unique functions, operating distinctly and yet as one. Similarly, there is *diversity* within the body of Christ. Christians are all different.

In Romans 12:6 we learn that Christians have received different gifts, and the measure of faith to go with each gift. In other words, if God gives a Christian a spiritual gift, he gives him sufficient faith to operate it. Can you imagine what would happen if God gave a person a particular gift and then not enough faith? It would be frustrating. So God matches the measure of faith with the gifts. But looking at I Corinthians 12:4 we read, "Now there are diversities of gifts." These are Spirit-given, divine gifts that each believer has. The body needs different gifts. Christians need to complement each other; no one can be everything. I am gifted to do one thing, someone else to do another, and we minister to each other for the body's health. Any organ that doesn't function maims and cripples the whole body.

And there are diversities of operation, but it is the same God which worketh all in all (I Cor. 12:6).

The body of Christ is marked by diversity and unity. Paul lists some examples of this principle in verses 7-10. He concludes by saying in verse 11:

But all these worketh that one and the selfsame Spirit, dividing to every man severally as he will.

In order to allow the body to function, so that all believers may minister to each other, the Spirit has apportioned the gifts in beautiful balance. If a Christian does not use his gift, the body is cheated. How does the diversity of gifts bring unity? As all believers are being ministered to and ministering their gifts in perfect exchange, they are all together maturing; the full complement of gifts is bestowed on every member.

Football players know that team unity is the basic ingredient in winning. Every player must carry out his assignment for the success of the whole. Imagine a sportscaster interviewing a player. The player says the team is one, really one, so much so that everyone has decided to play quarterback. That is not unity, it is chaos. The team doesn't need eleven quarterbacks. There must be diversity in the midst of basic harmony. The team needs ends, tackles, guards, a center, and backs. Each must be fully committed to his unique place on the team if there's to be unity. My coach used to say, "If you believe that your position is the most important one on the field, and if you play it that way on every play, we can't be beaten!"

Diversity is vital to the functioning of the church. Spiritual gifts are a sovereign, God-given blessing. A Christian must use his. He may say, "Well, I applied to the Sunday school and they don't need a third grade teacher." That shouldn't stop him. The Bible doesn't say, "Find an organization and assign your gift to it." Since every believer has some spiritual gift, he can find a place to use it. There are many opportunities all around, in the church program and outside it. If a Christian has the gift of helps, for example, he may find someone who needs help—he doesn't need the church organization. If he has the gift of teaching, he may find a class and teach it, even if it is a class of one or two children in his neighborhood. He can find someone who needs to be taught. Many Christians are idle, though they have spiritual gifts that the body of Christ is craving. Someone needs every Christian to minister his gifts. The Spirit didn't give Christians their gifts just to lie on a shelf.

How can a Christian know his gift? By reading and studying the lists of gifts in Romans 12 and I Corinthians 12. Then pray and ask for the Holy Spirit's leading. His leading will confirm what the Christian likes to do and what he does with a measure of success and joy. If he loves to work with people, perhaps he has the gift of helps. If he is a good organizer, perhaps he has the gift of administration or ruling. If a Christian really wants to know his gift, the Holy Spirit will show him what it is. The Christian is not to become preoccupied, however, with the academics of gifts. If he is filled with the Holy Spirit, the Spirit's gifts will operate freely, and the Christian will be able to see clearly what his gift is by what the Holy Spirit does. Also, significantly, other members of the body will verify the gifts.

I was talking once with a Christian fellow, and said, "We have many needs among the people in our church. Could you help us? I've noticed you in our Bible studies." He said, "I'd love to help you, but I'm very busy. I have this Bible class, and I'm working with several people as well as some new Christians." I said, "Praise the Lord!"

A Christian doesn't necessarily need a church organization to minister his gifts. I've told my congregation, "You who are working here in the local congregation, this is where God has put you—use your gift. But if you find no opening, if there is no place for you in the structure as far as you know, just go and minister to someone. Go teach someone, go find someone who wants to know. This world is ripe. It is full of people who need to know the Word of God. You may strike up an acquaintance, meet with them, and just sit down and teach them some things. There are many new Christians who need to learn. Find a ministry. Don't wait for the structure; minister your gift."

The body of Christ must also have *harmony*. In the ministering of gifts there must be a harmonious blend.

UNITY

LOVE - HUMILITY - SPIRITUAL KNOWLEDGE

DIVERSITY

GIFTS - OFFICES - CALLINGS

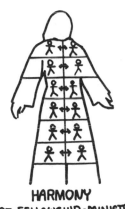

HARMONY

CARE - FELLOWSHIP - MINISTRY

PRACTICALLY

The body is one, a unity based on love, which is based on humility, which rises out of right spiritual knowledge. Yet it is diverse with different gifts, callings, and offices for each member. All are to interoperate in harmony. Practically, they do not, and the body is not the whole in practice that it should be.

If the foot shall say, Because I am not the hand, I am not of the body; is it therefore not of the body? And if the ear shall say, Because I am not the eye, I am not of the body; is it therefore not of the body? If the whole body were an eye, where were the hearing? If the whole were hearing, where were the smelling? But now hath God set the members every one of them in the body, as it hath pleased him. And if they were all one member, where were the body? But now are they many members, yet but one body. And the eye cannot say unto the hand, I have no need of thee: nor again the head to the feet, I have no need of you. Nay, much more those members of the body, which seem to be more feeble, are necessary: And those members of the body, which we think to be less honourable, upon these we bestow more abundant honour; and our uncomely parts have more abundant comeliness. For our comely parts have no need: but God hath tempered the body together, having given more abundant honour to that part which lacked: That there should be no schism in the body; but that the members should have the same care one for another (I Cor. 12:15-25).

This passage shows the Christian's attitude of respect for each fellow member. Each Christian is to be content with his gifts and harmonize with the whole body. It is not always the most obvious gift that is most critical. A beautiful mouth is nice, a lung is necessary. So is a thumb.

In the body of Christ there is unity, diversity, and harmony. To be a healthy body, the church needs every Christian—not necessarily more structure or more organization. Rather, the church needs more body unity and more body ministry. That is what Jesus prayed for. Christian unity is the unity of the Spirit, not the unity of the denomination or the organization. There will be true church unity when Christians humble themselves, when they work for the interests of others, when they love with a love that doesn't care about what happens to them, and when they begin to minister their gifts in harmony.

Chapter Two

GOD'S ETERNAL MASTER PLAN

Our discussion of the body of Christ will focus on its practical aspects, those which are part of the believer's life on earth. But the body of Christ transcends time, for it was formed in the timelessness of eternity by the sovereign design of almighty God. Initially, we must look at that.

The epistle to the Ephesians describes both the doctrine of the body and its practical life. In fact, the body idea is the pervading theme in the book. Paul says in 1:9, 10 that God has

made known unto us the mystery [sacred secret, hidden in the Old Testament] of His will ... That in the dispensation of the fulness of times he might gather together in one all things in Christ.

In addition, 3:3, 5 says:

How that by revelation he made known unto me the mystery ... Which in other ages was not made known unto the sons of men, as it is now revealed unto his holy apostles and prophets by the Spirit.

What is the mystery? Verse 6 tells us the mystery is "That the Gentiles should be fellowheirs, and of the same body." Then verse 9 reveals Paul's mission "to make all men see what is the fellowship of the mystery." This is the mystery of the body—fellowship. Paul was to declare that mystery (Eph. 6:19), that Jew and Gentile have been gathered together and molded into a single body, of which Christ is the head. God is forming a body of Jew and Gentile, rich and poor, learned and unlearned, male and female, slave and free—"one new man" (Eph. 2:15). This is the mystery of the body, unfolded in Ephesians. We will look at Ephesians to see these features.

Before any of us was born, before the earth was formed, God planned the body of Christ (Eph. 1:3-6a). Paul ascribes the forming of the mystery body to eternity past. A mystery in the biblical sense is a truth which God ordained in eternity past and hid, to be revealed at a certain time. A biblical mystery, then, must have a beginning in eternity past; so that is where Paul begins his presentation of the body.

There is a timbre of excitement in Paul's pen! Let's face it: to realize that God loved me and placed me within the body of Christ in His own master plan, before the world was even created, is cause for rejoicing. It is a glorious thought that God knew me by name before the world began and counted me a part of His blessed church.

Thinking of all these fantastic truths caused Paul to burst out in a great, long paean of praise (Eph. 1:3-14), which is all one sentence in his Greek writing. It may be the longest sentence in religious literature: 202 Greek words. It is connected, yet disconnected. It is a complicated sentence, so it must be taken piece by piece.

This lyrical song of praise flows from Paul's heart. His mind goes from glory to glory, from gift to gift, from wonder to wonder, and on and on. He talks about election, sanctification, foreordination, adoption, acceptance, redemption, forgiveness, enrichment, enlightenment, inheritance, the sealing of the Holy Spirit. All the cardinal doctrines are included in his song of praise, as he cites the facts about God's forming the body before the world began.

He constantly gives God the glory: "to the praise of the glory of his grace" (v. 6); "that we should be to the praise of his glory" (v. 12); "unto the praise of his glory" (v. 14). So you and I and every believer in Jesus Christ were components of a divine plan before the world began. Believers are in the body because God's eternal plan put them there. No wonder Paul praised God.

The song of praise actually has three parts: (1) Verses 4-6a deal with the past aspect of God's eternal formation of the body. "According as he hath chosen us in him" (v. 4). (2) Verses 6b-11 deal with the present aspect. "In whom we have redemption" (v. 7). (3) Verses 12-14 deal with the future aspect. "In whom also we have obtained an inheritance" (v. 11). God's eternal plan for the body has three parts: the past—election; the present—redemption; the future—inheritance. In this chapter we will discuss the past.

In Ephesians 1:4-6a Paul presents seven facts about God's formation of the body in eternity past. Seven is often God's number for perfection and completion. Paul reveals (1) the method by which the body was elected; (2) the objects of God's election; (3) the time of election; (4) the purpose of the body; (5) the motive for God's election; (6) the result of His election, and (7) the goal of it all.

1. *The method by which God formed the Body.* Paul writes, "According as he hath chosen us in him..." (1:4). That describes the method. He didn't draw straws; He chose by His sovereign will who would be in the body of Christ. Election was His plan. The Greek root for "chosen" is *eklego,* meaning

"to call out" or "to elect." He chose totally apart from human will and purely on the basis of His sovereignty. The Greek verb for "chosen" is in the middle voice and thus reflexive; the resulting meaning is "According as he hath chosen us for Himself." God acted totally independent of any outside influence. Paul's heart overflowed at such a glorious realization; he blessed God for choosing us—vile, unworthy sinners.

God wrote out the names in the book of life before the world began. Revelation 17:8 says,

> The beast that thou sawest was, and is not, and shall ascend out of the bottomless pit, and go into perdition; and they that dwell on the earth shall wonder, whose names were not written in the book of life from the foundation of the world (cf. Rev. 20:15).

God, by name, masterplanned you and me into the body of Christ by His choice. Election is the first cause of all blessing; that is why Paul begins with it.

The doctrine of election runs through the whole Bible. God does everything according to His own will and mind. Israel was elect (Exodus 6). The angels were elect (I Timothy 5). Christ was elect (I Peter 2). Certain believers were elected for certain tasks (Acts 9:15). The forming of the body is by election, by God's choice.

This principle is stated clearly in several passages. Jesus said to His disciples, "Ye have not chosen me, but I have chosen you, and ordained you" (John 15:16). Note John 1:12, 13:

> But as many as received him, to them gave he power to become the sons of God, even to them that believe on his name; Which were born, not of blood, nor of the will of the flesh, nor of the will of man, but of God.

Also, II Timothy 1:9:

> Who hath saved us, and called us with an holy calling, not according to our works, but according to his own purpose and grace, which was given us in Christ Jesus before the world began.

Then, II Timothy 2:10:

Therefore I endure all things for the elect's sakes, that they may also obtain the salvation which is in Christ Jesus with eternal glory.

Finally, II Thessalonians 2:13:

But we are bound to give thanks alway to God for you, brethren beloved of the Lord, because God hath from the beginning chosen you to salvation.

Despite some Christians' fears, these statements of God's election of believers are not in the Bible to cause a controversy. Election is a fact. It does not exclude the responsibility of man. It does not exclude personal response by faith. Jesus said, "Him that cometh to me I will in no wise cast out" (John 6:37). You say, but those two concepts don't go together. You're right. However, they both are true separately —election and human responsibility—and they form a paradox. But there is no paradox in the mind of God. He understands it perfectly; we don't. Our faith and salvation rest entirely upon the election of God, and yet the day a person comes to Jesus Christ, he comes because he desires to. Note the entire verse in John 6:37: "All that the Father giveth me shall come to me; and him that cometh to me I will in no wise cast out."

If salvation depends upon man, then praise to God is ridiculous. If it depends on us, we deserve to sing, "Praise me, glory to me in the highest." But, in truth, our praise to God is all the more appropriate because in forming the body before the world began, He chose us by a sovereign decree apart from works of man. How we must praise Him for that! The doctrine of election allows God to be God.

How can God choose some, offer salvation to everyone, and then hold people responsible who weren't chosen? I don't know. But the mystery is on our side. I don't know how God figures it out, but I am not going to worry about it. The Bible teaches election *and* human responsibility. I have heard people say that the truth is somewhere in the middle. Not so! The truth is at both extremes. There is no way to blend election and free will and get a mish-mash in the middle. Let God be God and man be man. I say, praise God for His secrets. His method, then, in forming the Body was election. I get excited knowing that God loved me before I was born. Maybe that is why He loved me!

2. *The objects of God's election.* "According as he hath chosen us ..." Who are the "us"? Please remember this, God didn't choose everyone to salvation. The Bible never teaches that. The "us" in this verse are Christian believers. Jesus says, in John 6:39, "And this is the Father's will which hath sent me, that of all that he hath given me I should lose nothing." There is a body which God has chosen to be a gift to Jesus Christ. Every believer is part of that love gift to Christ. He is the gift of a Father's love to His Son.

Romans 9:11 says,

For the children being not yet born, neither having done any good or evil, that the purpose of God according to election might stand.

God actually determines salvation before the children are born. To those who claim that this is unjust, Paul answers in verses 14, 15:

What shall we say then? Is there unrighteousness with God? [Is this unfair?] God forbid. For he saith to Moses, I will have mercy on whom I will have mercy, and I will have compassion on whom I will have compassion.

In verses 18 and 19 Paul states,

Therefore hath he mercy on whom he will have mercy, and whom he will be hardeneth. Thou wilt say then unto me, Why doth he yet find fault? For who hath resisted his will?

Why would God find fault in us if He didn't choose us? Paul's answer is,

O man, who art thou that repliest against God? [You have no right to question God.] Shall the thing formed say to him that formed it, Why hast thou made me thus? (v. 20).

Does the clay jump up and ask the potter why it looks the way it does? Not at all. You say, "Well, that is terribly cold and calculating." But that is just one side of God's sovereign election. Go to the next chapter in Romans.

Romans 10:9 reads,

That if thou shalt confess with thy mouth the Lord Jesus, and shalt believe in thine heart that God hath raised him from the dead, thou shalt be saved.

Do you read election in that verse? No, it is not there.

For with the heart man believeth unto righteousness; and with the mouth confession is made unto salvation. For the scripture saith, Whosoever believeth on him shall not be ashamed.... For whosoever shall call upon the name of the Lord shall be saved (vv. 10, 11, 13).

How these two sides of the truth come together is not a problem for us to resolve—it is God's! I don't understand it, I just rejoice in it. Christians, then, are the objects of the eternal election of the Body.

3. *The time of God's election of the body.* Paul says it was "before the foundation of the world" (Eph. 1:4). In eternity past God laid out all the plans. God must have had a marvelous time just mapping out the whole thing. This verse applies here: "Known unto God are all his works from the beginning of the world" (Acts 15:18). How much did God have planned? Everything. He formed the body in eternity past. He also planned the kingdom entirely in eternity past. He knew what the kingdom would

be. "Then shall the King say unto them on his right hand, Come, ye blessed of my Father, inherit the kingdom prepared for you from the foundation of the world" (Matt. 25:34). He laid the whole plan at once; the coming of Jesus Christ was part of it. "But with the precious blood of Christ, as of a lamb without blemish and without spot: Who verily was foreordained before the foundation of the world" (I Pet. 1:19, 20). In Revelation 13:8 Christ is called "the Lamb slain from the foundation of the world." God mapped it all out.

4. *The purpose of the body's election.* Why did God do it?

According as he hath chosen us in him before the foundation of the world, that we should be holy and without blame before him (Eph. 1:4).

God wanted us to be "before him," in His own presence. God wanted our fellowship. The whole body of Christ was designed for one thing—fellowship with the Father (cf. John 14:3; 17:24).

Man must meet some prerequisites if he is to have fellowship with God. Holiness is one. God chose believers to make them holy, that they may enter His presence. Anything unholy is removed from God's presence. Ephesians 5:25-27 says,

Christ also loved the church, and gave himself for it; That he might sanctify and cleanse it with the washing of water by the word, That he might present it to himself a glorious church, not having spot, or wrinkle, or any such thing; but that it should be holy and without blemish.

God chose us to purify us, so that we might have fellowship with Him. The purpose of His eternal election was to create a fellowship, a fellowship with God. Man could have that fellowship only if he were holy. So, God had to make us holy; He had to redeem us in Christ and give us Christ's holiness.

40

Paul also says Christians were chosen to be "without blame." The Greek word *amomos,* which Paul uses here, is used of a perfect lamb brought to the temple sacrifice. Man must be spotless to have fellowship with God. How many men have lived spotless lives? One—Jesus Christ. So God had to give to Christians the spotlessness of Christ. In Christ we become blameless and holy, so we can go before God and enjoy fellowship with Him. Those who love Him are now in that fellowship.

Election doesn't carry us halfway, but all the way to God. Some have taught that God elects you—that gets you halfway—and then you believe and get the rest of the way. I've heard that God casts a vote for you, the devil casts a vote against you, and you cast the deciding vote. No! That would make man, God, and the devil all equal. Election takes you to holiness; it makes you without blemish, cleansed from every sin like a perfect sacrifice brought into the presence of God.

5. *The motive of God's election.* Why did God do all this? The answer is found at the end of verse four and the beginning of verse five: "In love: Having predestinated us." Love motivated the formation of the body. Love generated election. The church didn't even exist. And that is the character of God's love. Human love is selective; it looks around and says, "Now there is a nice object. I will love that thing." But God's love is just there. God's nature is to love. Love was God's motive. We love Him only because He first loved us. In love, He predestinated us.

Some people see predestination as harsh, cold doctrine. No! It came from the warmth of God's love. The whole world deserved hell; only love chose us. Look at your sin and worthlessness, then remember that even before you existed, God loved you and chose you. "Herein is love, not that we loved God, but that he loved us" (I John 4:10). He loved us and

41

set His love upon us. It is exciting beyond words to know that God loves me and has loved me since eternity past—that is security.

> Come, ye blessed of my Father, inherit the kingdom prepared for you from the foundation of the world (Matt. 25:34).
> All that the Father giveth me shall come to me . . . of all that he hath given me I should lose nothing (John 6:37, 39).

6. *The result of election.* God set His love upon His own before the world began. When you love someone, you naturally want him as close to you as possible. You want the warmth of his love and his fellowship. Thus God loved us so much that He made us His children, the closest He could possibly get us to Himself, adopting us into His family. Adoption is the result of election.

Paul says this: "In love He predestined us in Jesus Christ for His sonship" (Eph. 1:5, Berkeley). That is as close as God could get us to Himself. Second-class sons? No. Hebrews 2:11 tells us Christ is not ashamed to call Christians his brethren; Romans 8:17 indicates we are joint-heirs with Christ.

In Roman days, when a child was adopted, he received every right of a born son. If a person was in debt or in trouble for crime, the moment he was adopted into a Roman family everything in his past was wiped clean. He had no debts; he owed nothing to society; his crime was forgotten; he started a brand new life. Everything his new father possessed was rightfully his.

Galatians 4:4-7 expresses this joyous truth:

> But when the fulness of the time was come, God sent forth his Son, made of a woman, made under the law, To redeem them that were under the law.

Why did He want to redeem us?

> That we might receive the adoption of sons. And because ye are sons, God hath sent forth the Spirit

of his Son into your hearts, crying, Abba, Father. Wherefore thou art no more a servant, but a son; and if a son, then an heir of God through Christ.

Does that not give the believer some insight into his identity? When God says the believer is a son, it means something. All the Father's love, all His spiritual blessings belong to the Christian. The Father's care and the Father's gifts are his; boldness to enter the Father's presence and to say "Father" in an intimate way; the promise of an inheritance; a place in the Father's house; all the rights and privileges of sonship. All this is true of every Christian because God formed a body in eternity past and chose sons to be adopted into His family.

7. *The goal of election.* Why did God do it? In the ultimate sense, what does it mean to Him to have us as sons? The answer is in Ephesians 1:5, 6: "According to the good pleasure of his will, to the praise of the glory of his grace." Verse 12 gives the same goal: "The praise of his glory." That is the reason for everything. The theme runs throughout the Bible: God's glory. "For it is God which worketh in you both to will and to do of his good pleasure" (Phil. 2:13). Christians are a real joy to the heart of God.

Believers need to understand that they are not just insignificant people worth very little, "lucky" even to be in the body. They are specially loved by God, chosen before the world began to be His body, to receive His love and blessings, and radiate Christ to the world.

Paul warns in Romans 12:3 that a Christian ought "not to think of himself more highly than he ought to think," but most Christians think too low. Something is wrong in a Christian's life if he doesn't in every day bless the name of God for what he is and has in Christ. How pathetic it is for a Christian with these glorious possessions and privileges to dabble in sin and disobedience! A Christian has no cause for a defeatist, inferior attitude. He is beloved by God, part of the body formed before the world began, master-planned into God's redemptive history. Outside the Trinity, he is the hottest commodity in the universe!

Chapter Three

KNOW YOUR POSITION

When I was playing college football, the coaches constantly drilled us with the admonition, "Play your position!" They had to say it often because when you see the action going on somewhere else on the field, you're tempted to dash over and try to grab the guy with the ball. Suddenly, with the coaches screaming, "Play your position!" the play would reverse and move into the spot you had just left.

One of the best ends on our team was so aggressive that he never stayed in his place. He was everywhere on the field tackling people, invariably the wrong ones. Finally he was benched. As good an athlete as he was, he proved worthless to the team because he wouldn't play his position.

There's a parallel to this in Christian experience. God has put us on His team and given us both the resources and the obligation to play our positions in the body of Christ. He gives us spiritual gifts for carrying out our assignments. In the football team's locker room the coaches diagram plays on a chalkboard. Everyone's position is plain to see. The plays always develop perfectly on the chalkboard, because the figures representing the players always make the right moves. On the field it's a different story.

The Christian must first find his position in Christ. He must study the chalkboard, so to speak, and see where he stands, who's on either side of him, who's behind him, who's in front of him. He cannot be an effective participant in Christian experience until he learns his place. Many Christians don't know how to live partly because they really don't know their position.

In Ephesians the Apostle Paul takes the first three chapters to present the believer's position, the spiritual standing that God has given him in Christ. In the last three chapters Paul tells how "to play the game." Once a Christian really knows his position, his resources, and his power, he can get into the game wholeheartedly with confidence that he can do the job. Otherwise, he will not function properly.

Basically, God's gift of salvation in Christ brings a believer into a position of righteousness. Man naturally is a sinner, separated from a holy God. But God provided a common ground in Jesus Christ. By virtue of his faith in Christ a person can come to know God. Christ's perfect righteousness becomes the believer's.

The believer, of course, although declared positionally righteous, still has problems in his life. He has not become personally or practically righteous 100 percent of the time in his own experience, but he is nevertheless righteous in his positional standing before God. The believer is exhorted, then, on the basis of his position to strive for righteousness in practice.

This theme runs right through the New Testament: Christians are to become in practice what they are in position. These positional statements in the Scriptures describe every believer: spiritually alive unto God, dead to sin, forgiven, righteous, a child of God, God's possession, an heir of God, blessed with all spiritual blessings, a citizen of heaven, a servant of God, free from the law, crucified to the world, light to the world, victorious over Satan, cleansed, holy and blameless, set free in Christ from the power of sin, secure in Christ, knows peace and rest, indwelt by the Holy Spirit.

"Well, I certainly don't act like it!" you say. That's why, in the New Testament, for every positional statement there's a corresponding practice which Christians are enjoined to follow. For example, since the Christian is spiritually alive to God, he is told to live that new life; since he's dead to sin, he's not to give sin any place in his life; since he's forgiven, he's to count on it and not go through life feeling guilty; since he's righteous, he's to live righteously; since he's a child of God, he's told to act like God's dear child; since he's God's possession, he's supposed to yield to Him; since he's an heir of God, he's to add to his inheritance.

God requires that a Christian live a life that matches what He has done for him. If believers would honestly study their position, their lives would be changed. They would understand that failure in some aspect of Christian living doesn't mean they lose their whole position. In truth, a Christian's position is forever settled, unchanging, permanent. Sometimes a believer thinks that when he's done something wrong, he's blown the whole thing, he's no longer righteous before God, no longer holy, his position somehow altered. That is false. Growth and maturity never touch a Christian's position.

On the other hand, just as stumbling will not change a Christian's standing for the worse, neither will growth add to it for the better. Some people hold that the more mature you become in Christian experience, the more God likes you; as you grow, God becomes more gracious and loving. But God's favor does not depend upon our works. God

hath saved us, and called us with an holy calling,

not according to our works, but according to his own purpose and grace, which was given us in Christ Jesus before the world began (II Tim. 1:9).

God's total grace was extended before the world was created. We can't add one wit to His favor. From the moment of our salvation we received the absolute favor of God—there's no degree to it.

The Christian is "accepted in the beloved [Christ]" (Eph. 1:6). He cannot subsequently increase or decrease in the favor of God. Nothing a Christian does, or fails to do, can change to the slightest degree his perfect standing before God.

When a normal baby is born, he has all his parts. He doesn't begin life with one leg, for example, then grow another leg in two years and a nose eight months later. The growth process doesn't add new parts, but merely strengthens existing ones. That's how it is with Christians.

When a person is created anew in Jesus Christ, he is created with all the necessary parts—nothing is missing. Christian growth doesn't add to us, but strengthens practically what God has positionally made us.

> I know that, whatsoever God doeth, it shall be forever: nothing can be put to it, nor anything taken from it (Eccl. 3:14).

When God does a work, it's done and we don't add and we don't take away. Instead of asking God for more parts, instead of seeking to be more favorable to God, we should do what the Apostle Paul prayed that the Colossians would do:

> give thanks unto the Father, which hath made us meet [fit] to be partakers of the inheritance of the saints in light (Col. 1:12).

The Christian is already fit and needs no other parts. No attainment, no growth makes him any more favored or more complete. Colossians 2:10 says simply, "Ye are complete in him." Paul here is not speaking of the Christian's practice; he doesn't say the Christian is perfect in behavior. But because of salvation, the believer is complete in Christ.

Hebrews 10:14 says, "For by one offering he (Christ) hath perfected forever them that are sanctified." When Jesus died, He made Christians positionally perfect forever in holiness. They lack nothing. They are eternally secure, perfect in Christ; their position never changes.

Yet a person who understands his position will see changes in his life. That's why in Ephesians, and elsewhere in the New Testament, the emphasis is on the believer's identity and his understanding of his positional resources. The appeals to certain standards of moral and ethical behavior always relate to who the Christian is: positional identity. A Christian with a healthy self-image will be an effective Christian. The mature Christian understands who he is, relies on his positional resources, checks them out, knows what's at his disposal, then charges into the practical aspects of Christian living.

In Ephesians 4:1 Paul says,

I therefore, the prisoner of the Lord, beseech you that ye walk worthy of the vocation wherewith ye are called.

The "therefore" refers to what Paul said in Chapter 3 about the believer's place: walk according to your position.

This reveals an interesting pattern in Ephesians. In 1:1-14 Paul speaks of the believer's position, and, as we shall note in more detail, in 1:15-23 he prays that we will understand our position. Again, in 2:1– 3:12 he gives positional truth; then in 3:13-21 he prays for the Christians to understand it. Twice Paul does it: position-prayer, position-prayer. Not until Chapter 4 does he get into the practice of the Christian life. The principle in Christian living, as in football is: you can't play your position until you know what it is. The Christian life is becoming what you are, becoming in practice what you are in position.

Paul's prayer in Ephesians 1:15-23 includes both thanksgiving and petition.

> Wherefore I also, after I heard of your faith in the Lord Jesus, and love unto all the saints, Cease not to give thanks for you, making mention of you in my prayers (vv. 15, 16).

Paul was in prison in Rome, but received reports from Ephesus. It had been four years since he was there, but Christian travelers using the network of Roman roads and sea transportation could easily bring him word. Paul and these people felt a sincere bond of love. The Ephesian believers would be concerned about his arrest, and they would want dearly to see him. Paul's heart was full of rejoicing, especially for two things he had learned of the Ephesians: their faith in Christ and their love for one another.

The two key ingredients are faith and love. True faith issues in love for the brethren. Love reveals that faith is genuine.

> He that saith he is in the light, and hateth his brother, is in darkness even until now. He that loveth his brother abideth in the light, and there is none occasion of stumbling in him. But he that hateth his brother is in darkness, and walketh in darkness, and knoweth not whither he goeth, because that darkness hath blinded his eyes (I John 2:9-11).

A prominent characteristic of the believer is his love for other believers. Love is a test of genuine faith. If a so-called believer has hatred for other Christians, he's really a counterfeit. The true believer has what Peter calls "unfeigned love of the brethren" (I Pet. 1:22). So the faith of the Ephesians matched that standard; it was genuine because it issued in love.

After assuring the Ephesians of his thankfulness for them, Paul's prayer becomes a petition that they might understand their position in Christ. The ignorance of many Christians is tragic. The prophet Hosea noted this: "My people are destroyed for lack of knowledge" (4:6). They were cut off from blessing because they didn't know the facts. Many Christians stumble throughout their lives because they have no idea what their resources are. They don't know their identity.

What is more, God gives the believer the equipment to understand his position and resources. The natural mind does not understand spiritual truth. If the brain were the key to spiritual understanding, the most intellectual persons would be the most Christlike. But note what Paul prays for:

That the God of our Lord Jesus Christ, the Father of glory, may give you the spirit of wisdom and revelation in the knowledge of him (Eph. 1:17).

As Paul might well have said, "I want you to understand your resources, and you can't understand them on your human level; you have no natural capacity for it—it's a supernatural ability that comes from God."

The key to the verse is the word "spirit." Is it the Holy Spirit? He may not pray for God to give them the Holy Spirit, because they have already received Him—at the time of their conversion. "If any man have not the Spirit of Christ, he is none of his" (Rom. 8:9). If you don't possess the Holy Spirit, you are not a Christian. The moment you receive Christ, the Holy Spirit comes to live in you.

Is Paul speaking of the so-called human spirit? Hardly. How could a man be given a human spirit when he already has one? So what does Paul mean? If it's neither of those, perhaps it's both. Let me explain:

The Greek word for "spirit" (pneuma) means many things: wind, breath, air, spirit. But it also means an attitude, disposition, or influence. We may read Ephesians 1:17 this way: "I'm praying that God will give

51

you the attitude of wisdom and revelation." We use "spirit" that way in our day; someone comes into the room looking gloomy and you say, "You're really a sad spirit today." You don't mean he has a human spirit, the Holy Spirit, and a sad spirit; you mean his prevailing attitude. Or, you may say, "Look at that guy! Boy, is he spirited!" You don't mean he has a human spirit, the Holy Spirit, and an activated spirit; you mean that's his attitude, his disposition.

Paul is asking God to have the Holy Spirit work on the human spirit to produce an attitude that is concerned about wisdom and revelation in the knowledge of Him. We must understand our resources. So Paul prays, "Give them an attitude, a disposition that's preoccupied with understanding the wisdom and revelation of the knowledge of God."

The highest thing a Christian may do in this life is give himself unstintingly and wholeheartedly to a constant study of "wisdom and revelation." The Spirit is essential to produce the right attitude in the believer and enable him to understand God's revelation.

> But God hath revealed them unto us by his Spirit; for the Spirit searcheth all things, yea, the deep things of God. For what man knoweth the things of a man, save the spirit of man which is in him? even so the things of God knoweth no man, but the Spirit of God. Now we have received, not the spirit of the world, but the spirit which is of God; that we might know the things that are freely given to us of God (I Cor. 2:10-12).

It takes the Holy Spirit to work on us, to create in us an attitude that hungers to know our resources. Every Christian needs the disposition that hungers and thirsts after the knowledge of God.

The Christian, of course, knows God through his faith in Christ. Paul's concern is for a depth of knowledge, which takes more than human intellect. The Holy Spirit alone can unearth the mine of the deep things of God and open the Christian's mind to

52

understand them. The two aspects of such understanding: "wisdom and revelation." Revelation refers to the facts, wisdom to the practical use of facts. The apostle considers both the content and the proper use of knowledge. There's a vast difference between "a knowledge of spiritual things" and "spiritual knowledge." Many people know a lot of theology. But there's more: wisdom to apply the facts, which is spiritual knowledge. Some degree of divine illumination comes with salvation, but every Christian needs a clearer, stronger spiritual vision to plumb the deep things of God. But what deep things, what resources does Paul want them to see? Three, basically: (1) the greatness of God's plan; (2) the greatness of His power; (3) the greatness of His Son.

1. *The greatness of God's plan.*

The eyes of the understanding being enlightened; that ye may know what is the hope of his calling, and what the riches of the glory of his inheritance in the saints (Eph. 1:18).

When a Christian has "the spirit of wisdom and revelation" in his heart, his inner spiritual capacity for understanding the truth is enlarged, and he will have a greater grasp of the plan of God than he had before. Paul describes this process as having "the eyes of your understanding ... enlightened." The word translated "understanding" is the Greek word *kardias,* meaning "heart." It refers to the inner man. The inner man must be enlightened to understand the hope of God's calling and the riches of His inheritance.

This enlightenment has nothing to do with IQ, but rather, spiritual sensitivity to the Holy Spirit. I know people on the lower rungs of the ladder academically who have keen spiritual insight. On the other hand, I've met some on the top of the academic ladder who lack any spiritual insight. We see the principle of spiritual enlightenment in several Scriptures:

> These are the words which I spake unto you, while I was yet with you, that all things must be fulfilled, which were written in the law of Moses, and in the prophets, and in the psalms, concerning me. Then opened he their understanding, that they might understand the scriptures (Luke 24:44, 45).

These verses describe the process between Jesus and His disciples. Divine intervention alone can unlock our spiritual understanding. The natural man cannot do it; the truths about God's plan must be supernaturally revealed.

Lydia provides another example:

> And a certain woman, named Lydia, a seller of purple, of the city of Thyatira, which worshipped God, heard us: whose heart the Lord opened, that she attended unto the things which were spoken of Paul (Acts 16:14).

Who opened her heart? The Lord. She could not understand the spiritual truths Paul was preaching apart from the Holy Spirit's work in her heart.

Paul explains the principle in II Corinthians 4:4, 6:

> The god of this world [the devil] hath blinded the minds of them which believe not, lest the light of the glorious gospel of Christ, who is the image of God, should shine unto them. . . . For God, who commanded the light to shine out of darkness, hath shined in our hearts, to give the light of the knowledge of the glory of God in the face of Jesus Christ.

Knowing the truth is the result of God making light shine within us. That's why Paul prays in Ephesians for the inner man to be enlightened spiritually.

Two aspects of God's plan, Paul stresses the believers should understand: the hope of His calling, and the riches of His inheritance.

The little phrase, "the hope of His calling," ranges from eternity past to eternity future, covering everything in between. "Calling" refers to God's election of the believer before the foundation of the world (Eph. 1:4). Our "hope" is eternal life with Christ.

Paul, in effect, prays that Christians will understand God's election in eternity past, His glory in eternity future, and all He has given the believer in between. In a word, the hope of our calling wraps up everything God has given the believer in his salvation. The security of God's plan is revealed in I Thessalonians 5:24: "Faithful is he that calleth you, who also will do it." Our hope, our assurance is that He will do what He says He will.

This is the answer to a spiritual inferiority complex. In the plan of God the believer was chosen, redeemed, made holy, and glorified. He said He would do it, and He did it. His word assures our position in Christ and our resources. The secret of a proper Christian self-image is not to have an exalted view of ourselves, but the right perspective as we stand in Christ. It is a critical matter in spiritual growth; the Christian needs to know who he is. To find out, to explore the depths of your position in Christ, you need the hunger for spiritual insight, which the Spirit of God can produce in your spirit as you search the Word of God.

The second aspect of God's great plan for enlightening believers is "the riches of the glory of his inheritance in the saints." Saints, in the biblical sense, are those who have called upon Christ in faith (I Cor. 1:2). In God's master plan He has given believers an inheritance; all that God has is ours—endless riches for eternity. We are "joint-heirs with Christ" (Rom. 8:17).

It's impossible to describe precisely "the riches of the glory of his inheritance." Whatever it is, we know it is more than any one will ever need. There is no bottom, no end to it. Indeed, in Ephesians 3:8 Paul calls God's riches "unsearchable." But that doesn't keep him from talking about them—he mentions "the riches of his grace" (Eph. 1:7); God being "rich in mercy" (2:4); and "the riches of his glory" (3:16).

God's riches are adequate for any situation a Christian may face. But how can the believer find his resources. Colossians 3:16:

Let the word of Christ dwell in you richly.

If one's mind is saturated with the Word of God, the unending resources will begin to flow. This is the answer to fear, doubts, and anxiety: understanding your resources because you were picked to be a part of God's plan. His plan is right now for every believer, because each one is not just "in" God's plan, he *is* God's plan. Thus it is essential to have spiritual understanding of your position.

All my life I heard what I ought to do for God. I was told to be more dedicated, more committed, more consecrated; I was always being enjoined to do this, do this, do this. I got so frustrated I wondered if God had done anything for me; I wanted someone to say, "Here's what God wants to do for you." This is the great blessing of knowing our position in Christ, knowing all that's ours because we *are* God's plan. So Paul prays for the believers to understand the greatness of the plan.

2. *The greatness of God's power.*

And what is the exceeding greatness of his power toward us who believe, according to the working of his mighty power, Which he wrought in Christ, when he raised him from the dead, and set him at his own right hand in the heavenly places (Eph. 1:19, 20).

It's not enough to speak of the greatness of God's power; it is "exceeding greatness." Paul puts into verse 19 every word he can think of that means power. Best of all, that power is right here—"toward us"—not out there in the cosmic universe. But what is that power?

"Power" in Greek is *dunamis,* from which we get our word "dynamite." God's power in the believer is so great he is like a walking stick of dynamite. Christians ought to be exploding all over this world. Instead, many don't even fizzle; they never bother even to light their fuses. They don't know that in Christ they are literally *dunamis*.

This power is "working," which is the Greek word *energeia*, from which we get our word "energy." Christians are energized by almighty power, absolute power, the power that created the universe. Paul describes it as the power God used when He raised Christ from the dead and put Him at His right hand. Many Christians wonder if they've ever experienced such power. Yet that same power was unleashed in the Christian at the time of his conversion, as Acts 1:8 confirms:

> But ye shall receive power, after that the Holy Spirit is come upon you.

The Holy Spirit comes with His power at the time of our salvation.

> Buried with him in baptism, in which also ye are risen with him through the faith of the operation of God, who hath raised him from the dead (Col. 2: 12).

God's power raised Christ and exalted Him in heaven. That same kind of power is exhibited in the believer, according to this verse, which tells what happened to the believer when he received Jesus Christ. God showed his resurrection power at the point of the Christian's salvation; God made him alive in Christ. That was the first thing that happened—God's power was unleashed. What a tragedy if that power lies dormant in the believer subsequent to his conversion.

> Whom we preach, warning every man, and teaching every man in all wisdom; that we may present every man perfect in Christ Jesus: Whereunto I also labor, striving according to his working, which worketh in me mightily (Col. 1:28, 29).

The Christian has God's power; it belongs to him.

57

Paul shows how this power worked in his life as he labored to preach and teach Christ. His energy came from God. Paul knew God's power practically in his own experience; thus he could speak of the Gospel's coming to Thessalonica "in power" (I Thess. 1:5).

God's resurrection power, seen in the believer's salvation, is in his life and available for use now. Too many Christians, asked to do something for Jesus Christ, fumble around and wonder if they can handle it. It is sad for a Christian to suffer from an emasculated image of himself. Get a grip on who you are. You are supercharged with divine dynamite; why chug along in your Christian life at five miles an hour, when you may get into it with your throttle wide open. If you doubt that, see Ephesians 3:20:

Now unto him that is able to do exceeding abundantly above all that we ask or think, according to the power that worketh in us.

It would have been great enough if Paul had said, "Now unto him who is able to do that we ask." Or, if he had said, "Him who is able to do *above* all we can ask or think," that would be greater. Or, if he had said, "Him who is able to do *abundantly above* all we can ask or think," we might be content to stop there and try to take it in. But Paul goes on to define God's power at work in us as being "*exceeding* abundantly above all that we ask or think." It was this power Paul desired—"That I may know him, and the power of his resurrection" (Phil. 3:10)—and the power he experienced—"I can do all things through Christ which strengtheneth me" (Phil. 4:13). The same may be true for every Christian!

3. *The greatness of God's Son.*

Far above all principality, and power, and might, and dominion, and every name that is named, not only in this world, but also in that which is to come (Eph. 1:21).

That speaks of the Lord Jesus Christ, who is in the believer. Christ is far above: all principalities—a rank of angels; power, might, and dominion—another rank of angels; every name that is named. Nothing in the universe is higher than Jesus Christ; the angels holy and fallen, Satan, every power, every authority, every name in all history, every name that's yet to be—none is superior to Him.

> And hath put all things under his feet, and gave him to be the head over all things to the church, Which is his body, the fulness of him that filleth all in all (Eph. 1:22, 23).

This is a symbolic reference to the king elevated above his subjects, who bow before him. It is the climactic picture of the believer's position in Christ. The Christian does not operate independently in this world; he is part of Christ's body, the church of which Christ is the head. All life flows from Him; each member functions in Him.

Knowing how the church stands in Christ, why should she not be moving dynamically in the world? The head needs the body to carry out its work; the body needs the head for direction.

When young Timothy was having his problems—with older people giving him such a hard time that he got stomach trouble—Paul told him directly, "Remember Jesus Christ" (II Tim. 2:8). Yes, he was to take a little wine for his stomach trouble (perhaps an ulcer), and he was to stir up his spiritual gifts. But when he was at the end of his rope, Paul gave him the supreme counsel: Look to your resources in Christ.

Paul did not tell Timothy to rededicate or reconsecrate himself. Timothy needed to take a fresh look at Jesus. "Remember," he said, "Jesus Christ, born of the seed of David"; that's the humanity of Jesus. "Remember Jesus Christ . . . raised from the dead"; that's His deity.

When a Christian gets into difficulty, he needs to remember Christ's sympathetic understanding and divine power. There is no excuse for misunderstanding who Christ is.

In the Old Testament, when the prophet Habakkuk was discouraged, he had to step back and simply look at who God is. Habakkuk had a real problem because Israel needed spiritual revival; and God's answer was to send judgment through the Chaldeans. Habakkuk was confused and angry. How could God use an ungodly nation to punish His people? Habakkuk thought he had God in a box, but God reaffirmed His plan and Habakkuk had to back off the problem and see himself in the right perspective. He told the Lord, in effect: "I don't understand the problem. I just know that you are a good God who never makes mistakes, that you are of purer eyes than to behold iniquity, and even if everything goes the opposite way I would like to see it go, and my whole world collapses, I am going to trust you" (cf. Hab. 1:12, 13; 3:18, 19).

That is the way to solve every problem. The Christian must forget the problem, take a stand on firm ground, and remember who Jesus Christ is and what He came to do. Remember who is in you. There is no place for fearful, lukewarm believers. Do we really know our resources, the greatness of God's plan and our place in it? Truly, every believer needs a spirit of wisdom and revelation in the knowledge of God's plan, His power, and the person of Jesus Christ.

PRACTICING YOUR POSITION

In Christ we are perfect positionally; but in practice we fall short of perfection. The Christian life is the experience of becoming in practice what we are in position. This study sheet shows that for every positional truth in the New Testament there is a corresponding practice we are enjoined to follow.

POSITION What we are II Pet. 1:3, 4 / Eph. 1:3 Col. 2:10 / Heb. 10:14	EXPERIENCE Acting like what we are II Pet. 1:5-8 / Eph. 4:1 II Tim. 3:17 / Col. 4:12 Heb. 13:20, 21
1. *Spiritually alive to God* Eph. 2:1, 4, 5 / I John 4:9 / John 11:25 John 14:19 Acts 17:28	*Live the life* Phil. 1:21 / Gal. 2:20 (Rom. 6:11-13) Titus 2:12
2. *Dead to sin* Eph. 1:7 / I John 1:9 1 John 2:12 Rom. 6:2-10	*Give no place to sin* Rom. 6:11-15 / Col. 3:3
3. *Forgiven* Eph. 1:7 / I John 1:9 I John 2:12 / Col. 1:14	*Count on it!* Rom. 8:1, 33, 34
4. *Righteous* Rom. 1:17 / 3:21-26 4:1, 6 / 5:17	*Live righteously* II Tim. 2:22 / I John 3:7
5. *Children of God* Eph. 1:5 / Gal. 3:26	*Act like God's children* Eph. 5:1 / I Pet. 1:13, 14
6. *God's possession* Eph. 1:4 / II Tim. 2:19	*Yield to God* Rom. 12:1 / II Tim. 2:19-21
7. *Heirs of God* Rom. 8:17 / Col. 1:12 Eph. 1:11, 14, 18 I Pet. 1:3, 4	*Add to your inheritance* Matt. 6:19-21 II Cor. 5:9, 10 / II John 8 I Cor. 3:12-14
8. *Blessed with all spiritual blessings in the heavenlies* Eph. 1:3 / 2:6, 7 (II Pet. 1:3, 4)	*Set your love on those things* Col. 3:1, 2

9. *Heavenly citizenship (Not of this world)* Phil. 3:20 John 17:14-16 I John 5:4, 5	*Live as a citizen of heaven* I John 2:15 / Col. 3:1, 2 James 1:27
10. *Servant of God* I Cor. 7:22, 23 Rom. 6:22	*Act like a servant* Rom. 6:17-19 / 12:11 Heb. 12:28
11. *New life* II Cor. 5:17	*Walk in new life* Rom. 6:4
12. *Free from law* Rom. 6:14 / 7:1-6	*Yet keep fulfilling the law* Gal. 5:1 / Rom. 8:4
13. *Crucified to the world* Gal. 1:4 / 6:14, 15	*Avoid worldly things* I John 2:15-17 / James 4:4 Rom. 12:2
14. *Light to the world* I Thess. 5:5 Matt. 5:14	*Walk as children of light* Eph. 5:8 / Matt. 5:15, 16
15. *Victorious over satan* Rev. 12:9-11	*Claim your victory* Eph. 6:11-17 / James 4:7
16. *Cleansed* John 15:3 I John 1:7, 9	*Cleanse yourself* II Cor. 7:1 / Phil. 4:8
17. *Holy and without blame* Eph. 1:4 / I Cor. 3:17	*Live holy lives* I John 3:7 / I Pet. 1:15, 16 II Pet. 3:14
18. *Free* John 8:32	*Enjoy your freedom* Gal. 5:1
19. *In Christ* Eph. 1:3, 10 / 2:6, 13	*Abide in Him* I John 2:28
20. *Secure in Christ* I Pet. 1:5 / Rom. 8 John 10:27, 28	*Enjoy that security* II Pet. 1:10
21. *Possessors of peace* Rom. 5:1 / 14:17 John 14:27 Acts 10:36	*Follow after peace, let it rule* Rom. 14:19 / Col. 3:15 II Tim. 2:22 / I Thess. 5:13
22. *One* Eph. 4:4-6 / 1:9, 10 I Cor. 12:13	*Live that oneness* Eph. 4:3 / John 17:21, 24

23. *In Grace* Rom. 5:1	*Grow in Grace* II Pet. 3:18
24. *In fellowship* I John 1:3-7	*Experience that fellowship* I Cor. 10:20 / Eph. 5:11
25. *Joyful* Rom. 5:2	*Experience that joy* I John 1:4 / John 15:11 16:24 / Phil. 4:4
26. *Spirit indwelt and led* I Cor. 6:19, 20 Rom. 8:9 / 8:14	*Yield to the Spirit's control* Eph. 5:18 / 4:30 I Thess. 5:19 / Gal. 5:25
27. *Spirit — gifted* I Cor. 12:12, 4 Rom. 12:5, 6	*Use your gift* Rom. 12:3-6 / I Pet. 4:11
28. *Empowered for service* Acts 1:8 / Eph. 3:20 II Cor. 4:7 II Tim. 1:7	*Claim and demonstrate that power* I Cor. 2:4 / Phil. 3:10 Eph. 6:10 / Phil. 4:13
29. *Love* Rom. 5:5 I John 2:5; 5:1	*Love!* I Pet. 1:22; 4:8 John 13:34, 35 /I John 3:18

Chapter Four

SALVATION: ENTRANCE TO THE BODY

A young, handsome Muslim from India responded when I, addressing a group of Hollywood movie people, invited those desiring to receive Christ as personal Savior to talk with me afterward. When I told him how to trust in Jesus for salvation, he prayed and committed his life to Christ. Then he stood up, shook my hand, and said, "Isn't it wonderful! Now I have two gods—Jesus and Muhammad."

I explained his error. To him, knowing Christ was like going up to the shelf of life and saying, "I'll have one of those, and one of those, and three of those, and a little of Christ." It was a pick-and-choose kind of thing. But his confusion was no worse than that of many Americans when it comes to understanding what a Christian really is. "What is a Christian?" you may ask people, and you will get strange answers: a person who lives in America, or loves his mother, or goes to church, or is basically a good, moral type.

Because of this confusion we must analyze the true answer carefully. As clearly as anywhere in the Bible, the answer comes in Ephesians 2:1-10. We've seen that Ephesians is concerned with the mystery of the body: the body of Christ, the company of believers constituting the church. We've considered what it means to be in the body, when it was formed, and what our resources are—the power that Christians have because of their place in God's marvelous plan.

At this point in his letter to the Ephesians, the Apostle Paul pauses to review how believers came into the body. In Chapter 2 he writes not of the formation of the body in eternity past by election, but of how that plan unfolds in time and history. Paul tells in Chapter 1 how God planned that men would become part of Christ's body, how He would be the head, and how He would work through them. He writes in Chapter 2 about how God's plan becomes active in every individual who enters the body. How do we enter the body? There is one way—Jesus Christ. Paul reveals six facts about salvation in Ephesians 2:1-10: it is (1) from sin (2) by love (3) into life (4) with purpose (5) through faith (6) unto good works.

1. *Salvation is from sin* (Eph. 2:1-3). I talk to many people who think they are saved but have not turned from sin. There is no saved man who has not turned from sin. This does not mean he becomes sinless, but his life pattern has changed from a pursuit of sinfulness to pursuing godliness. It must be that way, for the Scripture says, "If any man be in Christ, he is a new creature: old things are passed away; behold, all things are become new" (II Cor. 5:17).

Man's sinful state and practice are clearly described in Ephesians 2:1-3:

> And you . . . who were dead in trespasses and sins; Wherein in time past ye walked according to the course of this world, according to the prince of the power of the air, the spirit that now worketh in the children of disobedience: Among whom also we all had our conversation in times past in the lusts of our

flesh, fulfilling the desires of the flesh and of the mind: and were by nature the children of wrath, even as others.

The natural man comes into the world spiritually dead. He is alienated from the life of God. Man's basic problem is not being out of harmony with his fellowmen, but being alienated from the life of God. Man is activated not by spiritual impulses from God but by bodily impulses.

I visited a home where a baby had died a half-hour earlier. The body was still warm. No stronger stimulus exists in humanity than that between a mother and her baby. But that mother could not revive her baby, no matter how hard she tried. Death means you can't respond; it means total inability to respond, whatever the stimulus. That is how man is born into this world, spiritually; he cannot react to the stimulus of divine truth because the inner man is dead. He cannot sense the impulses of the divine world; he cannot feel the heartbeat of spiritual reality.

The natural man might sit in a church wondering what other people get out of it. He may read the Bible and say, "Man, that's weird stuff! I don't understand it at all." A Christian tells him how wonderful his life is, now that he's living for the glory of God instead of for himself, and the natural man says, "Wow, you've given up everything that's really fun in life!"

One day as some men talked about following Jesus, one said,

Lord, suffer me first to go and bury my father. But Jesus said unto him, Follow me; and let the dead bury their dead (Matt. 8:21, 22).

Jesus' response brought to light physical and spiritual death. This potential disciple wanted to put off following Christ until his father died, because then he could cash in on the inheritance. His father was still living. But Jesus replied, in effect, "Let the spiritually dead bury the physically dead." There are two kinds of death: death of the body which we know as physical death, and death of the inner man, spiritual death, the state of every person when he's born.

Paul defines spiritual death as an active condition: "in trespasses and sins." Man is spiritually dead not "because of" sin but "in" sin. Man is not a sinner because he sins; he sins because he is born sinful. So, besides man's inner spiritual death—his insensibility to spiritual impulses from God—he is aggressively involved in sinning.

Two words describe man's sinful condition. The Greek word for sin is *hamartia,* which literally means "to miss the mark." You shoot an arrow at a target and it falls short. The mark, of course, is God's perfect standard of righteousness; everyone fails to reach it. As Paul notes in Romans 3:23,

> For all have sinned, and come short of the glory of God.

Many persons have a false concept of sin. They think of murder, robbery, rape, and drunkenness as sin, but they don't think of the average "good guy" as a sinner. Sin is not necessarily violent, but simply a failure to come up to the standard. A man may reach the mark of human goodness often; but since he cannot reach the mark of God's perfect holiness, he is still a sinner.

It's easy to confuse human goodness with the godly kind. Jesus said, "If ye do good to them which do good to you, what thank have ye? for sinners also do even the same" (Luke 6:33). There's a sense in which sinners do good to each other, if others do good to them. That's human, civic good. Shipwrecked at Malta, Paul noted, "The barbarous people shewed us no little kindness" (Acts 28:2). People motivated by human goodness donate their blood, food, money for charitable purposes. But civic, humanitarian goodness cannot compare with God's spiritual goodness.

The Scriptures say,

There is none righteous, no, not one; there is none
that understandeth, there is none that seeketh after
God. They are all gone out of the way, they are
together become unprofitable; there is none that doeth
good, no, not one (Rom. 3:10-12).

The "good" referred to here is godly good or
spiritual good. The best a natural man may do is
humanitarian good on a man-centered level.

The second word Paul uses to describe man's spiritual condition is *paraptoma* ("trespasses"). It once
meant a slip or a fall but came to mean traveling on
the wrong road. So, in spiritual terms, it means going
other than God's way. God says, "This is the way,"
but man says, "Sorry, I'm going to do my own thing."
The Bible states "There is a way which seemeth right
unto a man, but the end thereof are the ways of
death" (Prov. 14:12). Man not only falls short
(hamartia); he also goes in the wrong direction
(paraptoma). Man tries but misses and goes his own
way.

The unsaved man is dead in trespasses and sins.
He is spiritually insensible to God, can't feel godly
impulses, and doesn't understand God and divine
truth. The only thing left is to follow the appeals of
the world and the flesh. That's where his sensibilities
operate.

The person who cannot feel godly impulses will
fall victim to whatever is around him. Though his
spirit is insensitive, his flesh remains sensitive. Totally
sensitive in the body, he becomes the victim of bodily
desires.

This kind of life is described in Ephesians 2:2, 3.
The first characteristic is that it is lived "according
to the course of this world." An unsaved person does
whatever the world is doing. He walks the path that
the world system is walking. Whatever the world is
promoting, he is buying. He indulges in the sins of
the times. He is at home and in complete harmony

with the spirit of the age. There is always a prevailing spirit, an attitude, an influence that pervades the world, and unsaved people are captured by it.

The world system today, as I see it, is primarily selling humanism. Humanism says man is the ultimate end of everything: captain of his soul, master of his fate. Yet man can't figure out how to solve the tensions between parents and teenagers, between parents themselves, between workers and managers, between nations. Instead, man appears the victim of everything that's gone wrong: decaying cities, spiraling crime and divorce, air and water pollution, hunger and poverty, population explosion, and wars and threats of wars. Mankind is simply incapable of solving its problems by itself.

According to humanism, it's all right for everyone to do his own thing. The truth is, man at no time has done so. Why not? "In time past ye walked according to the course of this world, according to the prince of the power of the air" (Eph. 2:2). A person's life is controlled either by God or by Satan. When a man rebels against God and disobeys Him, he is not a free man; he is a slave to the prince of demons himself.

The word for "prince" in Greek is *archon*, which means the first one in order, in rank, the highest. Satan is the leader of a band of demons that inhabits the lower atmosphere. Scripture suggests there are three "heavens": the atmosphere around the earth, the stellar heavens, and the "heaven of heavens" where we'll abide with God. In the lower atmosphere encircling the earth this body of demons is activated and energized by Satan to corrupt men. The legions of hell surround the earth. That's why Paul says in Ephesians 6:12,

> For we wrestle not against flesh and blood, but against principalities, against powers, against the rulers of the darkness of this world, against spiritual wickedness in high places.

The battle is not just with men, but with the prince of demons and the host of his underlings.

Satan is active in the lives of unsaved people, energizing them to act on his behalf in his rebellion against God. The deeds of the unsaved are hatched in hell. Even an occasional good deed may be prompted by Satan to pacify a man's conscience so he will think he's really all right. Men are dupes in Satan's war against God. The devil is called a "roaring lion" in the Bible (I Pet. 5:8), devouring people and using them to fight against God's power and against godly principles in the world.

A second characteristic of the spiritually dead is that they are "sons of disobedience." This means their lives are characterized by disobedience. If an unsaved man is energized by Satan, he will disobey God; he is born that way. Thus children, without being taught, know how to disobey parents. In this life, then, a person constantly resists carrying out God's commands because whatever God tells him to do, Satan tells him not to do. For example, the Bible instructs a child, "Obey your parents," but Satan says, "Disobey." God tells husbands to love their wives, but Satan says, "Cheat on them, be unfaithful." The Bible tells wives to obey their husbands, but Satan tells them that's demeaning and old-fashioned. For everything God says, Satan says the opposite.

The third characteristic of the spiritually dead is that they live to fulfill physical desires selfishly. The Apostle Paul indicts Jews and Gentiles alike. The Gentiles (which most of the Ephesian Christians were) are the "ye" of verse 2, and the Jews are the "we" of verse 3. The raw paganism and immorality of the Gentiles and the hypocritical self-righteousness of the Jews are all called "the lusts of the flesh." The unsaved man is left to fleshly desires because his spirit does not receive godly impulses. Spiritually dead persons gain satisfaction from fulfilling such desires; for many, it is all they get out of life.

The Greek word translated "desires" is *thelema*, which can mean the desire for an irrational, forbidden thing. It suggests desire beyond the point of reason, beyond comprehension. It is marked by strong will. The outworking of *thelema* is described by Paul in Galatians 5:19-21: "Adultery" (sexual infidelity in marriage), "fornication" (other kinds of sexual immorality), "uncleanness" (impurity, a dirty mind), "lasciviousness" (wantonness, unrestrained abandonment to orgy), "Idolatry" (worshiping false gods), "witchcraft" (dabbling in the occult), "hatred," "variance, emulations, wrath, strife, seditions, heresies" (strife, jealousy, bad temper, selfishness, dissension, party spirit), "Envyings, murders, drunkenness, revellings." These are a catalog of what we see in human society today. It's because the inner man is dead.

The fourth trait of unregenerate man is that he is a child of "wrath." That means he is the object of God's judgment. Take a man who is dead in trespasses and sin, who follows the course of this world, who does what Satan wants, and seeks to fulfill the desires of the flesh, and you have a man who is dead center on the target of God's judgment. "The wrath of God is revealed from heaven against all ungodliness and unrighteousness of men" (Rom. 1:18). The principle at work in the universe is God's wrath against sin.

All of these traits relate to the basic truth: salvation is from sin, from both the state and practice of sinfulness as described above. Man is totally depraved, but salvation takes him out of that condition and changes everything.

2. *Salvation is by love* (Eph. 2:4). In man's condition, it requires love to reach him. He is certainly not lovable by virtue of his deeds and attitudes. Man's hopelessness can only be remedied if God intervenes. His intervention is reflected in the words, "But God . . ." The first three verses are a dismal picture indeed, but the story changes in verse 4. The ray of

71

hope we see for ourselves is God's breaking into the blackness of our condition with His love.

> But God, who is rich in mercy, for his great love wherewith he loved us (Eph. 2:4).

Staggering to contemplate, isn't it, that in view of our thoroughly rotten condition, God would still love us? But the giving of His love does not depend on how good we are. The character of God is to love.

God's love is shown in the richness of His mercy toward us. The man described in verses 1-3 needs nothing so much as mercy. If he got what he deserved, he would quickly be judged guilty, without hope. Instead it's as if God came into court and said, "You're guilty, but you may go free." If you ask Him why, He says, "Because I love you." On the other hand, God is also just. Does He discard His justice in this case? No, He puts it on Jesus. Thus Jesus had to die for sinners; He bore justice so the sinner could have mercy. Someone had to die, because the just penalty for sin is death. Once the justice of God was satisfied in Christ, God could extend His mercy to sinful man.

Perhaps we'd best think of mercy and grace as two sides of God's love. Mercy means not giving us what we deserve. Grace is opposite: giving us what we don't deserve. Mercy holds back judgment, grace gives pardon. By His mercy God says, "I'm not going to give it to you; I'll hold back judgment." By His grace God says, "I'll give you this in exchange; I'll give you salvation." Mercy withholds God's wrath, grace releases His forgiveness. Mercy pities us, grace pardons us. Only love can prompt mercy and grace.

Sometimes when my son Matt is disobedient, I say, "Matt, I have to spank you." At this, his lip quivers, his chin curls up, he reaches to put his hands on my face, and says, "Dad, I love you." My first reaction is to say, "Don't confuse the issue. I know you love me." But when he says, "Oh, Dad, I love you so much!" his deserved punishment goes out the window. I give him a hug and a kiss and say, "Try to shape up, will you?" It's honest, genuine love that breeds mercy.

Paul can't really describe God's love so he calls it "great love." But we can measure His love by the Cross. If we were to ask God to define His love, He might say this: "Do you see that rocky ridge outside Jerusalem? Do you see three crosses? The one in the middle has my Son. That's how much I love you." Man's sin is not so much a crime against God's law as against His love. There is a difference. Someone has illustrated it this way:

Suppose I drive down the street, run a red light, and hit and kill a little boy. I'm penalized for going through the red light and for manslaughter. I pay everything I owe to the state; it has no further claim on me. But it's a different story when I meet the boy's mother. It's one thing to pay a fine to the state for breaking the law; it's quite another to be made right in my relationship with the mother. I committed a crime against love, not just against the law. A sentence satisfies the law; only the wronged person's forgiveness may satisfy a crime against love. There's no price tag on that. For my crime against love I'm at the mercy of the person I've wronged. I must wait until that mother freely forgives me.

We break God's law and sin against His love throughout our lives. The only way we become right with Him is when God says, "I forgive you." Our salvation is the free act of His forgiveness, because He loves us.

3. *Salvation is into life* (Eph. 2:5).

Even when we were dead in sins, [God] quickened us together with Christ.

Christ comes in and makes the spiritually dead person alive. In that split second the dead becomes sensitive to God. The Word of God begins to speak to him. Christian love has meaning, and so does fellowship with other believers. He starts to look at the world in a different light.

Men need spiritual life, and Jesus says, "I'll give you that life, because I am that life. Being alive "together with Christ" means a person is identified in His death and resurrection. Paul said, "I am crucified with Christ: nevertheless I live" (Gal. 2:20). His death became mine when I received Christ, and I rose in newness of life. Because I identified myself with Him, my old life was put to death; because of His resurrection, I live.

Every Christian is totally identified with Christ. His life is not his own; Christ lives in him. He is no longer held in bondage by the desires of the flesh. He breaks out of the encirclement of sin and basks in Christ's freedom. That's what being spiritually alive means.

4. *Salvation has a purpose* (Eph. 2:6, 7). God had a purpose in mind when He planned salvation: "That in the ages to come he might show the exceeding riches of his grace in his kindness toward us through Christ Jesus." The believer died with Christ, rose with Him, and now lives a new kind of life. He actually sits together with Christ in the heavenlies; that is the new sphere of his spiritual existence. "For our citizenship is in heaven," declared Paul (Phil. 3:20, ASV). The Christian is living eternal life right now; He lives in a world where God is real and Christ exists.

Beyond that, the believer's future is secure because of what God has done for him in Christ. Paul uses the past tense in verse 6; he speaks of our already being in heaven. The Greek language has a unique feature; when the Greeks wanted to speak of things that were secure, they used the past tense. When they wanted to talk about something that couldn't change, that was inevitable, they expressed it in the past, as

74

if it had already happened. The Christian's place in heaven is secure because God guaranteed it.

God's purpose in this is simple to express: Christians will be His great trophies of grace, displayed before all the angels for eternity. God's glory, grace, love, and mercy are seen nowhere as great as in the lives of those He has redeemed. When we look at what we were before our conversion (Eph. 2:1-3), we understand why we are the greatest expression of His grace. We were at the bottom, but God gathered us up and placed us in heaven, so the angels might marvel at and praise Him for what He did in His redemptive plan (Eph. 3:10).

Everything exists for God's glory; thus He puts us on display. God receives the glory for what He has done in us. Someday, when we go bodily to heaven, we will show the host of heaven for eternity that God truly deserves glory. Revelation 7:9-12 gives us this picture of that event:

> After this I beheld, and, lo, a great multitude, which no man could number, of all nations, and kindreds, and people, and tongues, stood before the throne, and before the Lamb, clothed with white robes, and palms in their hands; And cried with a loud voice, saying, Salvation to our God which sitteth upon the throne, and unto the Lamb. And all the angels stood round about the throne . . . and fell before the throne on their faces, and worshipped God, Saying, Amen: Blessing, and glory, and wisdom, and thanksgiving, and honour, and power, and might, be unto our God for ever and ever. Amen.

Why were angels praising God? Because of His redemptive work. These people were the trophies of His grace, and they glorified God so much that the host of heaven broke out into joyful praise. Considering where we came from and what we will be, we ought never to stop thanking God for His wisdom, mercy, and love.

5. *Salvation is through faith* (Eph. 2:8, 9). Saving

faith is the gift of God. God gave us His love, mercy, and grace, and then the faith to respond. Faith in itself is not a human work that earns salvation; Salvation is "not of works," not even of faith as a work. God gives faith. If faith were of ourselves, we could say, "See, I had sense enough to put my faith in God." But, no, that would be boasting of works. Paul concludes that God gives us faith along with everything else. The spiritual realm opens to the dead natural man only when God in sovereign grace by a creative act opens the spiritual understanding. By faith, man responds to this act. This is spiritual re-birth, resurrection. By the miracle of regeneration a dead man becomes alive to the spiritual dimension and enters the mainstream of the life of God.

The spiritual truth may be illustrated by human birth.

When a baby is born, the doctor slaps his bottom and he begins to breathe. He breathes on his own. Smart baby! Baby knows if he's going to stay alive he has to breathe. No, the truth is, baby knows nothing. He breathes because he was whacked and felt pain. He instinctively cried. Why does a person breathe spiritually through faith? Because God, as it were, slaps him with divine grace. Faith is merely a response to the grace of God, which jolts someone into spiritual life.

Thus the Bible speaks of conversion as a new birth from above (John 3:3-8). New birth is a gift, which may not be earned. A baby can't bring itself into life. The same is true with spiritual life; God brings it into existence. All man does is start to breathe.

6. *Salvation is unto good works* (Eph. 2:10). Salvation is not by human works: confirmation, baptism, church membership, church attendance, communion, keeping the Ten Commandments, living by the Sermon on the Mount, giving to charity, or being a good neighbor. Doing one or all of these things will not

bring us from spiritual death to life. However, once a person is reborn by faith in Christ, his life is to be characterized by good works. We are saved "unto" good works, not "by" them.

A Christian is born to produce good works. He is God's "workmanship" (Eph. 2:10), a word which in Greek may mean "masterpiece." As God's masterpiece, the Christian has been formed to do good works; this work of God is a continuing process. God gives the believer new life in Christ; daily He is molding him into Christ's likeness.

A Sunday school teacher explaining Creation was irritated by one boy in the class. Thinking to shock the pupil, the teacher asked, "Who made you?"

"God did," the boy replied.

"Well, He didn't do a very good job!"

The boy retorted, "That's 'cause He ain't finished with me yet!"

In a practical sense, the boy was right.

The outworking for the believer is to walk in the good works that God has "ordained" for him. He is saved "unto" good works; now he is to do them. This is part of his salvation; it produces good works now. God has equipped His people to carry out His plan, which begins with the gift of faith and continues in the lifelong process of entering into good works. The Apostle John tells us the end of this process:

> Beloved, now are we the sons of God, and it doth not yet appear what we shall be: but we know that, when he [Christ] shall appear, we shall be like him; for we shall see him as he is (I John 3:2).

"We shall be like him" because God saved us from sin and death, giving us the life of Christ. He acted in love, gives us faith to respond to that love, designs good works for us to walk in, and plans to display us before angels. Such is the scope of salvation—entrance into Christ's body.

Chapter Five

RELEASING POWER IN THE BODY

Christian experience is a matter of applying God's power to the needs of everyday living. But many times Christians are frustrated because they don't know how to get God's power operating.

My car has a lot of power under the hood. But I must have the key, put it into the ignition switch, and turn it on, or none of that horsepower will do anything. If I know how every part of my car operates, and if every part is in perfect working order, I may say to my car, "Take me to the store," and it won't move. I have to use the key and turn on the power.

In our discussion of the body we have presented the Christian's power system, his resources. The body of Christ includes all true believers, with Christ as their head. The church as the body of Christ is a biblical mystery, something hidden in the Old Testament but revealed in the New. In Ephesians Paul describes the body: what it's like, how it functions, how the members interact. Chapters 1-3 gives the believer's position in the body. Chapters 4-6, his practice. Or, in 1-3 it's who the Christian is, and in

4-6 it's how he is to live. Elect before the foundation of the world, by the free grace of God, the believer enjoys forgiveness, redemption, and all spiritual blessings. He's part of God's great redemptive plan, a trophy of God's wisdom. He is one with Christ and with all believers. He is pure because of the blood of Christ. The great love of God reached down, took him just as he was in spiritual death, and transformed him. He is now God's masterpiece, created unto good works.

In this chapter we will discover from Ephesians 3:14-21 "how to stick in the key and turn on the engine." We start the engine here; the race doesn't begin until Ephesians 4.

Basically, this portion of Ephesians 3 is Paul's prayer that Christians know how to ignite God's power. The Christian has it; now he must learn to use it. There is a pattern of practical truth to help the believer work out his position. The prayer has five progressive steps: (1) inner strength; (2) the indwelling Christ; (3) incomprehensible love; (4) infinite fullness; (5) internal power. This passage unlocks the basic principles of Christian living. A believer who absorbs the pattern will revolutionize his life; knowing his identity will motivate him to action. From Paul's prayer we learn how to use God's power in our lives, how to experience His fullness.

1. *Inner strength* (Eph. 3:14-16). The first key to using the power is inner strength. For the proper setting we must connect Ephesians 3:1 to 3:14; verses 2-13 are a kind of parenthetical aside in Paul's thought. So we read, "For this cause I Paul, the prisoner of Jesus Christ for you Gentiles, . . . For this cause I bow my knees unto the Father of our Lord Jesus Christ." Paul repeats himself to show he is resuming his train of thought.

Paul bows to the Father for the reasons presented in Ephesians 1–2. God's eternal plan in choosing the

Body; His marvelous plan to redeem men, to make Jew and Gentile one in Christ, to exalt believers as a testimony to angels, to give them an inheritance. Bowing the knee is not simply for prayer but for worship and adoration. Paul seems driven to his knees by the sheer realization of all the resources he has in God's plan.

Verse 15 describes God as the Father "of whom the whole family in heaven and earth is named." One family. That is the emphasis in Ephesians—one body, one whole special family, God's family, all the redeemed, in heaven and on earth. The church comprises God's family because believers are His children. All believers "have access by one Spirit unto the Father" (Eph. 2:18); all comprise "the household of God" (Eph. 2:19).

Paul is about to request something, but he prefaces his request by acknowledging God as his Father. When a believer goes to God, he does not approach Him in the spirit of fear (Rom. 8:15); instead he cries, "Abba, Father," because he knows the Father loves him. He comes to prayer with boldness and confidence (Eph. 3:12). Paul prays that God will grant his request "according to the riches of his glory" (3:16). He asks that all God's attributes, all the depth of His glory, be at the disposal of the Christian. If a rich man gives you something "out of" his riches, it may be 25 cents; but if he gives you something "according" to his riches, it will be according to the outer limits of his wealth. God always gives that way. Salvation is "according to the riches of his grace' (Eph. 1:7). Paul's assurance was that God would supply all his needs "according to his riches in glory" (Phil. 4:19). A person's problem may be very serious, seemingly insoluble, but God's riches are infinitely available to him. In Christ they are "unsearchable" (Eph. 3:8), thus untraceable, inexhaustible.

On the basis of this wealth at his disposal, Paul

prays for strength "in the inner man" (3:16). How does it work? As the Christian yields his life day by day to the Holy Spirit, he gains strength within. The inner man is the inside man, the real you, the "I" that lives in your body. The outer man is the flesh, the physical body.

The Christian critically needs inner strength today, in view of the unique pressures of life: emotional and physical pressures that rip and tear at a person, knocking him off balance, leading to despair, discouragement, and hopelessness. A weak inner man can't stand the pressure.

If the inner man is weak, sin takes over and the believer can't resist it. He may become frustrated, guilty, and out of balance emotionally, mentally, and spiritually. The mental strain may lead to physical illness, because of their interaction.

However, it is possible for the Christian's inner man to be "strengthened with might" (3:16). Literally, this means "empowered with power." The supernatural power at his disposal is so great that Paul uses two Greek words to describe it, *krataio* ("to make strong") and *dunamis* ("power"). Such is the dynamic power available to the inner man.

Since the Holy Spirit strengthens the inner man (v. 16), we must know what the filling of the Spirit is. Though every believer possesses the Holy Spirit, some are weak inside. Filling occurs only as the believer yields himself to the Holy Spirit; this means turning life completely over to Him. It works like this:

Life consists of a host of decisions. Who will decide what to do? If a person is filled with the Holy Spirit, he says, in effect, "here's a decision I have to make. Show me the way to go." If he sees a temptation coming, he allows the Holy Spirit to meet it and defeat Satan. The Spirit-filled life is living in Spirit-awareness.

This relationship is not complicated. It is taking a

step at a time and letting the Holy Spirit be in charge. Being filled is in turn developed by the discipline of regular Bible reading and prayer. The mind of the Spirit is revealed in Scripture; in prayer the believer commits himself daily to the Holy Spirit.

Being filled is similar to a hand with a glove. By itself a glove does nothing; but if I put my hand into it, the glove is under its control. The glove doesn't argue and resist; it moves under the control of my fingers. The glove's only strength is my hand. The only strength a Christian has is the Holy Spirit.

Paul could pray for believers to be strengthened internally, because God had done it for him. God told Paul, "My grace is sufficient for thee; for my strength is made perfect in weakness" (II Cor. 12:9). Paul accepted that principle of divine working and rejoiced in it. He responsed to God:

> Most gladly therefore will I rather glory in my infirmities, that the power of Christ may rest upon me. Therefore I take pleasure in infirmities, in reproaches, in necessities, in persecutions, in distresses for Christ's sake: for when I am weak, then am I strong (II Cor. 12:9, 10).

How did this work out practically for Paul? When Paul left Ephesus for the last time, the Holy Spirit revealed that "bonds and afflictions" awaited him. He went ahead nevertheless, resolving:

> But none of these things move me, neither count I my life dear unto myself, so that I might finish my course with joy, and the ministry, which I have received of the Lord Jesus, to testify the gospel of the grace of God (Acts 20:24).

What of affliction? He faced it confidently in the strength of the Holy Spirit.

Paul recounted the sequel in his second letter to the Corinthians:

> With far greater labors, far more imprisonments, with countless beatings, and often near death. Five times I have received at the hands of the Jews the forty

lashes less one. Three times I have been beaten with rods; once I was stoned. Three times I have been shipwrecked; a night and a day I have been adrift at sea; on frequent journeys, in danger from rivers, danger from robbers, danger from my own people, danger from Gentiles, danger in the city, danger in the wilderness, danger at sea, danger from false brethren; in toil and hardship, through many a sleepless night, in hunger and thirst, often without food, in cold and exposure. And, apart from other things, there is the daily pressure upon me of my anxiety for all the churches (II Cor. 11:23-28, RSV).

What a catalog of experiences! Was Paul nervous and defeated? No, because he was strong in the inner man. He was strong because he was filled by the Holy Spirit and allowed Him to direct his life. Further testimony:

We are handicapped on all sides, but we are never frustrated; we are puzzled, but never in despair. We are persecuted, but we never have to stand it alone: we may be knocked down but we are never knocked out! Every day we experience something of the death of Jesus, so that we may also know the power of the life of Jesus in these bodies of ours. . . . This is the reason why we never collapse. The outward man does indeed suffer wear and tear, but every day the inward man receives fresh strength (II Cor. 4:8-10, 16, *Phillips*).

Paul says, in effect, "Man, the stuff that hits you on the outside, that's nothing, because every day we get renewed in the inner man with fresh strength." Only in the Holy Spirit did he have that kind of power. Surely the Christian will meet trouble, but he accepts the blows joyfully, knowing that God is working in his life with infinite patience and love, shaping him into His masterpiece.

So the first step to unleashing power in the body is to lay hold on inner strength by the Holy Spirit. That gets the key into the ignition. If the Christian is weak inside, nothing will happen.

2. *The indwelling Christ* (Eph. 3:17). Here is the

progress in developing power: as the inner man is strengthened by the Holy Spirit, Christ dwells in his heart. Paul doesn't say Christ "comes into your heart" —that's salvation. Rather, in verse 17, he writes to people who are already believers. He says, "That Christ may dwell in your hearts." The difference is between coming initially and dwelling thereafter. The distinction appears in the Greek word used for "dwell," *katoikeo,* which means literally "to settle down." It pictures coming into a home and settling down there. Result: when you are strong in the inner man, Christ, who is already there, settles down and feels at home. A believer must ask himself whether Jesus is comfortable in his heart. In some Christians there is so much sin and disobedience that Christ isn't at home.

Robert Munger, in his book, *My Heart Christ's Home,* gives a simple but vivid illustration of this spiritual principle.[1] He compares his heart to a home. Since Christ has come there to live, He asks to go through it. First He goes to the library—the control room, the brain where all the thoughts are, where information is stored. Jesus finds trash, evil, and untruth; it has to go, so the man cleans it all out. In the library there's to be a portrait of Jesus, a reminder that Jesus is there in the brain, at the center of his consciousness.

The dining room is next, the room of appetites and desires. Jesus asks him what he longs for; he wants the leeks, garlic, and onions of Egypt, all the worldly delights. Jesus says, "If you want food that really satisfies, seek the will of my Father. Your appetite should be to do His will."

When they enter the living room, Jesus says, "You know, I sit in the living room every morning and you come right through here so fast you never even stop

---

[1] Robert Munger, *My Heart Christ's Home.* (Downers Grove, Ill.: Inter-Varsity, 1954.)

to talk to me." The living room represents fellowship, conversation, sharing. Jesus says, "I've been a guest in your house, and you don't even talk to me. I want your fellowship."

In the workshop Jesus sees many toys the man has made with his tools. "Is that what you've done with your skills?" He asks. The point is, How do you use your talents, your abilities for the kingdom of God? If Jesus dwells in your heart, He controls this room, too.

Finally the man and his Savior return upstairs, only to encounter a strange odor coming from the hall closet. It represents secret sins. The man is upset; he figures if Jesus controls the dining room, living room, library, and workshop, that should be enough. But the odor persists; the clean house has a bad smell. Jesus asks him to open the closet door. It's full of rotten, dead things—things the man wanted to keep doing, things he didn't want to turn over to Jesus— but they have to come out.

Only when Jesus controls every room is He really at home in your heart. This comes about by the indwelling Spirit; His work is to extend the lordship of Jesus Christ to every part of the believer's life. This is the process: first you yield to the Holy Spirit; the result of being filled is strength in the inner man. As the inner man strengthens, Jesus cleans out your life and settles down there. In wondrous condescension, He is willing to leave the infinite majesty of heaven and make His home—actually feel at home—in your heart. Jesus said,

> If a man love me, he will keep my words: and my Father will love him, and we will come unto him, and make our abode with him (John 14:23).

Jesus wants to settle down in your life.

3. *Incomprehensible love* (Eph. 3:17-19). When Christ settles down and feels at home in a believer's

life, love grows everywhere. Using the metaphor of planting a tree, Paul says that when Christ dwells in your heart you are "rooted and grounded in love." Jesus said,

A new commandment I give unto you, That ye love one another; as I have loved you, that ye also love one another. By this shall all men know that ye are my disciples, if ye have love one to another (John 13:34, 35).

If the world fails to recognize Christians, it's because the Christians lack love for one another. God loves the world and wants to show that love through Christians. That happens only when the Christian yields himself to the Holy Spirit, is strong in the inner man, and allows Jesus to fill his life. The consequence: love will burst forth, because it is Jesus' nature to love. He will show His love if He has an open channel.

Peter echoes these thoughts:

Who by him do believe in God, that raised him up from the dead, and gave him glory; that your faith and hope might be in God. Seeing ye have purified your souls in obeying the truth through the Spirit unto unfeigned love of the brethren, see that ye love one another with a pure heart fervently (I Pet. 1:21, 22).

Before a Christian can love people fervently, he must be established in love. Before he can be established in love, he must have a pure heart. To have a pure heart he must resist temptation. To resist temptation he must be strong in the inner man. To be strong in the inner man he must be controlled by the Holy Spirit.

When you arrive at the Spirit-filled life, you are not at the end. That is the beginning. When you are filled with the Holy Spirit, things happen. When Christ settles down in your life, things happen. If a Christian says he doesn't love, it's because Christ isn't at home in his heart. Christ's isn't at home because he isn't strong in the inner man. He doesn't have a strong inner man because he's not filled with the Spirit. Love is simply the by-product of this spiritual process. And when a person is rooted and grounded in love, see what happens:

> That ye . . . May be able to comprehend, with all saints, what is the breadth, and length, and depth, and height; And to know the love of Christ, which passeth knowledge (Eph. 3:18, 19).

The only way to comprehend the love of Christ is to be rooted and grounded in it. There is only one thing that understands love—love. Someone asked Louis Armstrong about jazz, and the famous trumpeter said, "Man, if I got to explain it, you ain't got it." That's how it is with love. If a person has to tell you what it is, you are not rooted and grounded in it. Love is something only a lover can comprehend.

If you are a parent, and someone tells you, "You know, I really love my little child," you understand what they feel. But children themselves don't always understand that love. Some teenagers may not understand how much a parent can love, because they aren't parents.

"Comprehend" in Greek is *katalambano*, which means to seize something and make it your own. The only way you can seize the love of Christ and make it your own—understand it, comprehend it, look it over, see what it is—is to be rooted and grounded in it.

Paul prays that every believer—"all saints"—will comprehend Christ's love. Every believer is able. But that ability is latent in some; others don't understand it fully; some cheat themselves out of it because they are not rooted and grounded in love.

Christ's love is so great it is expressed in four dimensions: breadth, length, depth, and height. We may not grasp completely what Paul is thinking, but we may have some distinct impressions. Looking at

Christ's love is like looking at the endless universe. It's far out this way, that way, that way, and every way. Limitless love. It goes as far as "up" is, as far as "down" is, as far as "out" is. An early Christian used the cross as the symbol of this kind of love. The post points upward and downward ("height and depth"), the ends of the crosspiece point to the widest horizons ("breadth and length").

The letter to the Ephesians itself reveals a picture of the extent of Christ's love. *Its breadth* (2:16-18). Jews and Gentiles are made one, both are reconciled to God, both have access to the Father. The breadth of Christ's love reaches to the extremities of humanity, Jew on the one hand, Gentile on the other. *Its length* (1:4 and 2:7). It's as long as eternity past to eternity future. His love began before we were born. He chose believers "before the foundation of the world . . . in love." His love began in eternity past and keeps going through "the ages to come."

Its depth (2:1). Christ's love is so deep it reaches down into the pit of sin and spiritual death and pulls us out of it. We were at the bottom of bottoms, but Jesus rescued us in love. *Its height* (2:6). The believer has been raised to sit with Jesus in heaven. He has been lifted from the pit to an exalted position in glory.

Can a Christian understand the dimensions of Christ's love when faced with what looks like a disastrous situation? If he can, he may say to God, "I just can't wait to see how You will show me Your love in this." In every circumstance the believer, if he comprehends Christ's love, is able to say, "All right now, Lord, I've got a grasp of it. I grabbed it. I've looked at it. I see it." Such comprehension comes to him who is rooted and grounded in love. The development of spiritual power in the body, then is like this: strong inner man; Christ is at home; love radiates from your life; you comprehend Christ's love.

4. *Infinite fullness* (Eph. 3:19). What a fantastic truth: "filled with all the fullness of God"! I don't know if even Paul understood this entirely. Perhaps we can imagine him getting so excited about it that he jumps out of his chair before he actually writes it in his letter. How tremendous! First the believer is filled by the Holy Spirit, then by Christ, and now he has all the fullness of God.

Having the fullness of God means total spiritual maturity. It doesn't mean that all there is of God comes to live in the believer; that can't be. God does not move into you and limit himself to your capacity. No, it's like drawing a thimbleful of water from a lake. The thimble is filled with the lake, but you don't have the lake in the thimble. That thimble doesn't diminish the lake, yet it has the "fullness" of the lake in the sense that the thimble contains a particle of every ingredient of the water. All the essential character of that lake is in the thimble.

In the same way, when a believer has the fullness of God, he possesses the essential characteristics of God. But God is not diminished. The believer has a "thimbleful" of God's fullness, so he can communicate what God is like to the world. He's supposed to radiate God everywhere out of that fullness.

Since God is love, a believer filled with the fullness of God will express godly love. Since God is wise, a believer filled with the fullness of God will express godly wisdom. Since God is holy, the believer filled with the fullness of God will display holiness. Since God is gracious, a believer filled with the fullness of God will communicate godly graciousness.

Those attributes of God which are communicable He deposits in the Christian. The believer has what God is in reduced measure, so he can love with divine love, judge things with divine wisdom, and live with divine holiness—without being divine himself. In a word, to be filled with all the fullness of God is to be godlike: wise, just, holy, pure, loving, gracious, merciful.

Every Christian seeks a goal. Here it is: to be filled with all God's fullness. When he reaches that goal, people will see God's character revealed. We meet too few Christians who have reached it, but when we do we certainly recognize them. There's something attractive and powerful about a person who radiates the fullness of God.

This whole concept obviously staggers the mind. How could God take a worthless human being, a rebel against His love, and give him His fullness? Unbelievable. Yet it is true. The only thing to say is, "Thank You, God, for putting Your fullness in me. Thank You for helping me to radiate Your wonderful person."

If the world is to understand that God is love, where will it be seen? In Christians. If people are to recognize that God is wise, they must see God's wisdom in believers. Christians are responsible to communicate who God is not just by words, but by deeds.

5. *Internal power* (Eph. 3:20, 21). The concept in these verses is difficult to grasp. Lest we think having all the fullness of God is arrival at the summit, Paul now talks about unleashing God's power in our lives. Spiritual power is the power of God working in the believer.

That power becomes available to him who is filled with God's fullness. Possessing God's power means that in the believer God can do things "abundantly above" what the believer asks or thinks. God "is able to do ... according to the power ... in us."

Paul explains what he means in II Corinthians 4:7: "But we have this treasure in earthen vessels, that the excellency of the power may be of God, and not of us." God placed His power in our frail, insignificant, worthless bodies, so when anything does happen in the Christian we will know He is doing it.

It is thrilling to see this power at work when we are aware of our own incapacities.

What is the answer for a Christian who feels his life is a fizzle? Consider again the progressive development of power in the body of Christ. It starts with the inner man made strong by the Holy Spirit. Christ settles down and makes Himself at home in the believer. Consequently, the believer comprehends love. Then he is filled with the fullness of God, and power is released in his life. The result is beyond even what a Christian may dream God can do.

Finally, there's the goal of this process of spiritual development: the glory of God. Some Christians ask, "Why bother with all this? I'm going to heaven anyway." The answer is in verse 21. God wants to be glorified in the church *now*. That's the purpose for everything He does—His own glory. A Christian should not be content to think about heavenly bliss to the exclusion of glorifying God now. Happy and blessed is the believer who makes God's glory his goal. Every Christian should be able to say "amen" to Paul's prayer. That amen signifies, "Let it be so in my life." When God turns loose His power in the body, He will be glorified. The question is, Do we want that power, to glorify Him, and are we willing to work through these successive steps to obtain it?

Chapter Six

HIGH POSITION DEMANDS A LOWLY WALK

When a person joins an organization, like a lodge or a civic club, he obligates himself to live by its rules and standards. He gives himself to strive for its goals. He is expected to conform to what the organization stands for.

In the body of Christ conformity is expected also, not to rules and regulations, but to love. A believer calls himself a child of God, he has joined God's family, he belongs to his heavenly Father. This declaration shows he shares the goals of the body and wants to conform to what God requires. This is a conformity of love. If a Christian fails to conform to the pattern of he body, it's not because he lacks rules; he lacks love.

When the Christian entered the body, he received all rights, privileges, and honors (Ephesians 1-3). The consequence of this is to expect the believer to act like a member of the body. In Chapter 4 the Apostle Paul begins to write about the kind of behavior he expects of a Christian.

Ephesians divides this way. Chapters 1-3, doctrine; 4-6, duty.

Duty is the obvious response to doctrine. It is not a random response, but the only proper one. When a person knows the truth, the obvious thing for him is to act like it. The word "therefore" (4:1) is the link between doctrine and duty. Paul also makes this connection in Romans 12:1. After eleven chapters of doctrine, he says, "I beseech you therefore..." It appears also in Galatians 5:1, after four chapters of doctrine: "Stand fast, therefore...."

This is why the body needs consistent doctrinal teaching. Teaching only duty, without doctrine, weakens the counsel of God for the believer. It leads to a legalistic spirit or causes the believer to try to live on emotional pep talks. If doctrine is not taught, the believer lacks the true motive for Christian living. He needs the solid facts of the Word of God rather than human appeals to duty.

The New Testament itself constantly appeals for the teaching of sound doctrine. Paul says the Christian is "renewed in knowledge" (Col. 3:10). Knowledge, not emotion. Peter commanded, "Grow in grace, and in the knowledge of our Lord and Saviour Jesus Christ" (II Pet. 3:18). Knowledge is the key to good works (Col. 1:10). As Ephesians 1:17 indicates, the basis of a solid spiritual foundation is knowledge. Thus Paul takes three chapters of Ephesians to spell out doctrine.

A Christian's conduct is directly related to the extent of his knowledge. He may limp along because he is ignorant doctrinally; he may never dig into the Word of God. Then he may hear of a painless cure to his problem, something that usually involves an emotional charge of some kind, and he goes after a new feeling rather than sound doctrinal knowledge.

Paul has been careful to delineate basic doctrine. In Chapter 4 he begins to teach the characteristics of Christian living that match the believer's position. The transfer from doctrine to duty is a key New

Testament concept; it is a natural response. For example, in Colossians 3:12 Paul says,

> Put on therefore, as the elect of God, holy and beloved, bowels of mercies, kindness, humbleness of mind, meakness, longsuffering.

Because of his position, "the elect of God, holy and beloved," the believer is supposed to live a certain way. Or, Colossians 3:1, 2:

> If ye then be risen with Christ, seek those things which are above.... Set your affection on things above, not on things on the earth.

The believer's position is "risen with Christ." If that's true, he is supposed to do certain things. Duty follows position.

Earlier we noted the believer's high position. He is "blessed ... with all spiritual blessings in heavenly places in Christ" (1:3). He possesses "the unsearchable riches of Christ" (3:8). Chosen before the foundation of the world, he is redeemed and forgiven and enjoys God's inheritance. Once dead in trespasses and sins, he has been made alive in Christ. He is one in the body of Christ with every other believer. The Christian stands at the apex of God's magnificent work of love, mercy, and grace. Positionally, in Christ he is God's classic accomplishment. Except for God Himself, there is nothing in a more exalted position than the Christian. Now, we must ask, what kind of a "walk," what kind of behavior, what kind of life matches that position? A proud one? No, the believer's high position demands a lowly walk. After all, the believer himself had nothing to do with his position; it is all of God. The true Christian response to a high position is lowliness, meekness, longsuffering, in a word, humility.

Ephesians 4:1-6 includes: (1) the call to a "worthy walk"; (2) the characteristics of the worthy walk; (3) the cause of the worthy walk.

1. *The call to the worthy walk* (Eph. 4:1). The

Christian's "vocation" in this verse is not his job, his profession or his career, but his calling to salvation, to the body of Christ. Paul's appeal for a worthy walk is rooted in his status as a prisoner *in* Rome as he writes this letter. However, he never considered himself a prisoner *of* Rome, but a prisoner of the Lord. His bondage was in the plan of God. Paul was confident that God, not the Roman government, was in control of his life. Once he had been imprisoned in Philippi, and at that time God saw fit to deliver him. If God wanted him set free from the Romans, He could deliver him.

But how is Paul's appeal rooted in imprisonment? This way: he believes we should be loyal to our calling in Christ no matter what. Paul says, in effect, "Look, friends, I'm a prisoner. That's about as bad off as you can get, and I can still say, 'Walk worthy of your calling.' It may lead to jail, but that's not the important thing."

Paul himself is one who walked worthy of his calling, no matter what the price. He had been faithful to his trust; he had fulfilled his calling. It led to a Roman prison; regardless, he was loyal to his Lord.

But Paul was also passionately concerned for the spiritual welfare of those whom he had been called to serve. The depth of his concern is revealed in the words, "I . . . beseech you." This was not a legal command; it was an appeal grounded, of course, in the Holy Spirit's work in the believer, but also grounded in Paul's own spiritual convictions. He expresses this elsewhere:

Furthermore then we beseech you, brethren, and exhort you by the Lord Jesus, that as ye have received of us how you ought to walk and to please God, so ye would abound more and more (I Thess. 4:1).

For I have not shunned to declare unto you all the counsel of God. . . . Therefore watch, and remember, that by the space of three years I ceased not to warn every one night and day with tears (Acts 20:27, 31).

Why did he care so much? Because his purpose in life was to "present every man perfect in Christ Jesus" (Col. 1:28). Paul could not settle for less than total spiritual maturity in every believer to whom he ministered. This, I pray, will always be an ingredient in my ministry. It ought to be present in every Christian's ministry. Paul simply begged people to live out their Christian commitment. It was the passion of his life. And he was expendable in that effort.

Paul's burden should be the burden of every pastor. If he doesn't yearn with the depths of his being for the spiritual growth of his people, he should leave the ministry. A man called to the ministry must never cease to exhort his people toward spiritual maturity, the worthy walk. Such a servant of Christ was Epaphras, who labored fervently that believers would "stand perfect and complete in all the will of God" (Col. 4:12).

The word "walk" in Ephesians 4:1 describes the pattern of a Christian life, the Christian's daily conduct, his life-style. This idea occurs also in I Thessalonians 2:12: "That ye would walk worthy of God, who hath called you unto his kingdom and glory"; in Philippians 1:27: "Only let your conversation [conduct] be as it becometh the gospel of Christ"; and in Colossians 1:10, "That ye might walk worthy of the Lord unto all pleasing, being fruitful in every good work, and increasing in the knowledge of God."

Perhaps the best explanaton of this concept is found in a phrase Paul uses in his letter to Titus: ". . . that they may adorn the doctrine of God our Savior in all things" (2:10). Because the Christian's calling is "high" (Phil. 3:14), "holy" (II Tim. 1:9), and "heavenly" (Heb. 3:1), he is supposed to live by a certain standard of conduct. A godly life brings to light before men the various facets of God's transforming grace and love. A life of obedience to God, of holiness, humility, love, joy, and peace shines like so many precious jewels, adorning the Truth.

Suppose, for example, you try to explain to an unbeliever the truth about God. He's not so sure. Then one day he encounters, in a different way, a godly person. In his mind he sees not only intellectual truth, but the truth becomes attractive and appealing to him because he sees it in action. That's how a Christian, by his worthy walk, can adorn the doctrine of God in the eyes of the world. This is a serious responsibility, but it can be fulfilled. This was one key to the growth of the early church; it multiplied according to its godly walk (Acts 9:31). There would be a tremendous impact on the world today if all believers in the body adorned the doctrine of God by godliness in their behavior.

2. *The characteristics of the worthy walk* (Eph. 4:2, 3). Having urged the necessity of a worthy walk, Paul gives five characteristics of it: (1) lowliness; (2) meekness; (3) long-suffering; (4) forbearance; (5) unity.

"Lowliness" is genuine humility that comes from an association with Jesus Christ. The Christan's position is very high, exalted, but he walks at the very bottom. A Christian can know a lot of doctrine, memorize Bible verses, be faithful to the church, and be involved in many Christian activities, but if his life is not characterized by humility, his is not the worthy walk.

Pride is disastrous to Christian experience, but in the Greek world Paul knew humility was a joke. The word translated "lowliness" *(tapeinophrosune)* does not even appear in classical Greek; this expression was coined by Christians. The Christians introduced humility to the world of their time.

When a Christian looks for an example of humility, he need look only at Christ. His humility is described in Philippians 2:6-8. That description is prefaced in verse 5 with the admonition, "Let this mind be in

97

you, which was also in Christ Jesus." Real disciple-ship begins here.

What Paul cited as a characteristic of the worthy walk he himself exemplified. "Serving the Lord with all humility of mind, and with many tears, and temptations [trials], which befell me by the lying in wait of the Jews," Paul testified (Acts 20:19). This was his farewell statement to the elders at Ephesus, so when he wrote to them later they could recall the example of his life before them. Yes, he was often ambushed by his enemies, so to speak, but he per-severed with humility.

Humility really comes from proper self-awareness, Christ-awareness, and God-awareness. True humility comes hard because it begins only when we honestly face ourselves. Bernard said humility "is the virtue by which a man becomes conscious of his own un-worthiness." However, many people waltz through life with their minds behind a facade, because they don't have the courage to look at themselves and see what they really are. When you really face yourself, it is humiliating.

A person has no reason to exalt himself. Humility is taking off the rose-colored glasses of self-love and seeing just an unworthy sinner.

Humility is also built on Christ-awareness. This means measuring yourself by the right standard. A person may think he rates high as long as he puts himself against mediocre standards. For example, when I was in high school I received a gold trophy as "player of the year"; when I got to college I found out there were a lot of top players around. Next, I went to a pro football training camp, and there I saw that I was really nothing special compared with pro-fessional standards. In track I was good enough to win ribbons in my school; but when I got into the finals of the county invitational meet, all of a sudden the standard changed and I finished eighth. I was nothing compared with the big boys.

A Christian may look outstanding compared with the alcoholic who lives down the street. But godless neighbors are not the believer's standard; his standard is Jesus Christ. No matter how good a Christian thinks he is, when he puts himself up to Jesus, he doesn't come anywhere near Him. That is the road to humility.

God-awareness is a factor in humility. It is realizing that if it weren't for God, we wouldn't even exist. Humility is acknowledging that God controls everything. When a person becomes too proud, God often reaffirms His sovereign control in that life. When that happens, it's humbling.

The worthy walk starts "with all lowliness" and continues with "meekness." Meekness is the attitude of a person who submits to God's dealings without regret and to man's wickedness without revenge. The meek Christian says, "Well, if that's the way you want it, Lord, well, praise the Lord!" The meek person doesn't continually insist on his rights; he would rather take the wrong than inflict it on someone else.

However, a meek Christian is not a wishy-washy, spineless person. No, the meek person has true character and backbone. It takes more strength to allow yourself to be meek than it does to fight for your rights every time someone wrongs you. The meek person has courage and convictions. As Aristotle said, he is angry at the right time and not angry at the wrong time. If he's angry, it's because God is maligned, not because he himself has been hurt. The sufferings of others is his concern, but he doesn't get upset when he suffers.

Yet some Christians act like children, insisting on their rights all the time. If they are offended, they take their ball and go home. "I'm never going back to that church," they declare. We hear it often: someone offended me. Well, that is a good way to learn meekness.

As He exemplified humility, so the Lord Jesus Christ also showed what meekness is. When people rejected Him, He didn't quit and go home; He "endured the cross, despising the shame" (Heb. 12:2). Despite the wicked treatment He suffered at the hands of men, Jesus prayed, "Father, forgive them; for they know not what they do" (Luke 23:34). Meekness requires the greatest amount of fortitude in the time of crisis.

Meekness is really a spirit of submission. If it seems to be a downward step, remember how far down it was for Jesus. He was the one who made the world and sustains it. But He became the meek and lowly one, and set the pattern for a worthy Christian walk. Think what beauty and power there would be in the body of Christ if meekness and lowliness were the order of the day, with no one insisting on and fighting for his own rights but rather submitting himself to one another (Eph. 5:21).

The third component of a worthy walk is long-suffering. This is the spirit that never gives in. No matter how bad life gets, the long-suffering person keeps plugging away with endurance and persistence. Specifically, the word in Greek, *makrothumia,* refers to long-suffering in regard to people. It means taking whatever men dish out, bearing insult, injury, and complaint with patient endurance, without bitterness and irritation. The long-suffering Christian loves and waits.

The body of Christ needs the virtue of long-suffering. It often is fractured when some believer is offended and makes a big issue of it. Instead, he should endure the offense, remember the worthy walk, and press on as Jesus did. A Christian has no call to retaliate. Rather, he is called to lowliness, meekness, and long-suffering.

Paul describes the fourth characteristic of the worthy walk as "forbearing one another in love." This is the outworking of the first three. If the believer is humble, meek and long-suffering, he will not strike back when offended. Forbearance is accepting the mistakes of others and not being shaken by them. Forbearing one another means Christians loving one another, even though the other might offend. The Christian has room in his love to accommodate someone else's mistakes.

When offended, the forbearing believer says with patient love, "I know you didn't mean it. You shouldn't have acted like that, but that's all right, I love you." This kind of spirit instantly heals breaches in the fellowship of the body. Whenever there is a problem in the body, apply the salve of forbearance, a little tender love and affection.

Again, Jesus showed us on Calvary what forbearance is. He was forbearing in the face of slander, insult, and physical abuse. Jesus asks that the Christian who is wronged is to assume the same spirit He showed toward His persecutors. This attitude is described by Peter as "fervent charity . . . [which] shall cover the multitude of sins" (I Pet. 4:8). If I love only perfection, then I don't have Christian love. I must allow room for a brother to make a mistake, even toward me, and still love him.

When these four characteristics of the worthy walk —humility, meekness, long-suffering and forbearance —are in motion, the fifth one follows: "Endeavouring to keep the unity of the Spirit in the bond of peace" (Eph. 4:3). The bond which holds unity together is peace. Peace springs from love, love from humility. People can be at peace with each other because they love each other. The result of the worthy walk is unity, spiritual oneness.

The key to obtaining the fifth characteristic of the worthy walk is in the phrase "endeavoring to keep." We have to work at unity to keep it. "Endeavor" means putting forth an effort. Suppose we face some choices in a given situation. We decide one way and there's bound to be discord. Or we may decide another way that will lead to preserving unity in the body. Which should we choose? The way that will keep unity. Though you may have been wronged, you still do what you can to "keep the unity of the Spirit."

It is important that Scripture does not command Christians to *create* unity. God has already made them one body in Christ; rather than create unity, believers are to *keep* what they already have. They do so by following the pattern of the worthy walk Paul describes. We don't need more church conferences on unity, but we do need to encourage one another to live the kind of life that is lowly, meek, long-suffering and forbearing in love.

Acquiring these virtues in the Christian's worthy walk depends on one thing: death to self, submission of the ego. So long as self is at the center of life, so long as personal feelings and prestige have top priority, the worthy walk is unreachable. If self is first, God's doctrine is not adorned, a believer cannot be at peace with other believers, and the body will not experience oneness. All these things happen only when self dies.

3. *The cause of the worthy walk* (Eph. 4:4-6). These verses show the reason for the worthy walk: unity. God planned unity from the beginning. In these verses there are seven "unities," which comprise the basis for the lowly walk. The point is clear that believers should endeavor to keep unity visibly before the world, because that is God's own plan.

God gave one body, one Spirit, one Lord, one faith, one hope, one baptism. He is one God. These unities are the doctrinal foundation of the body.

One body. Christians are commanded to keep unity because there is one body of Christ. There are many local assemblies and congregations, but one body. There is not the Pittsburgh body, the Chicago body, and the Los Angeles body; the universal company of believers of all ages, races, and nationalities is the church, one body.

Although Christians differ in race, custom, culture, national origin, language, temperament, and other such qualities, they are all one in Christ. Jew, Gentile, intelligent, ignorant, educated, uneducated, rich, poor —they are one in Christ. Some in heaven, some on earth, but all believers from Pentecost to the Rapture of the church comprise Christ's one body.

The body's unity transcends the divisions of all human organizations. Admittedly, there are manmade factions. The body is not always seen as one outwardly; Christ's oneness is divided by human divisions. Denominational distinctives sometimes tend to fragment the body rather than unify it.

The genius of the one body is that it is not only universal and timeless, but it is also local and present. Each local congregation is to manifest the same unity within itself that the universal body is to show. The local church is not the whole body, but it is to be unified; as a part of the whole it is to function as a unit. That local unit has the necessary gifts to function as the body.

This unity is intended to be a witness to the world. Jesus prayed for believers to express their oneness "that the world may believe that thou hast sent me" (John 17:21). All Christians around the world are one body, and the practical expression of this oneness is a sign that the Father loved the world and sent His Son into it (John 17:23). Thus the need for an outward manifestation of inner spiritual reality is great today. If the church does not show true oneness, it appears to the world to be just another social organization with the same quarrels and divisions other groups have.

One Spirit. The Holy Spirit is the source of Christian unity, because he lives in every believer (Rom. 8:9). Every believer has Him in common. The body of Christ collectively is the dwelling place of the Holy Spirit, as well as individually.

Paul emphasizes this truth in Ephesians 2:22:

In whom ye also are built together for an habitation of God through the Spirit.

and in Ephesians 4:3:

Endeavoring to keep the unity of the Spirit.

This unity is based on the fact that the Holy Spirit is the agency of the new birth (John 3:5-8), and consequently comes to live in the believer (John 14:16, 17; cf. I Cor. 12:13).

Because of this we can test the reality of the Spirit's work according to unity. If something arises within the body that brings division, not unity, then we can be sure it is not of the Spirit. That is a very helpful test in this day, when people come and say that certain religious expressions are genuine. I say, "How do you know? Did it bring unity? If not, then it is not of the Holy Spirit."

This was the test applied in the Book of Acts. The Holy Spirit was the sign of spiritual validity. The Council of Jerusalem (Acts 15) was a debate over whether or not the Gentiles had really been saved without keeping the Jewish law. Speaking of the converted Gentiles, Peter said, "God, which knoweth the hearts, bare them witness, giving them the Holy Spirit, even as he did unto us" (15:8). The same Spirit-induced phenomena of Pentecost, such as tongues, accompanied the outreach of the Gospel to the Gentiles. At Pentecost the Holy Spirit came on the believing Jews at Jerusalem. Later on, when the Gospel went to the Gentiles, the Holy Spirit came upon them in the same way (Acts 8, 10).

Why did the Gentiles share the same experiences as the Jews did at Pentecost? God wanted the Jewish believers to know that when the Holy Spirit came upon the Gentiles, He came in exactly the same way as He did upon them; thus the outward sign of His coming—tongues—was the same. The Jewish believers had to be sure the Gentiles had received the same Spirit they did. There was to be unity. One part of the body could not say to another part, "We have something you don't have." The Holy Spirit is the common denominator in the body.

One hope. Every believer shares the same hope, even though the circumstances of his calling to that hope are different. Each member of the body is unique, but all share a common destiny, which is to be like Jesus Christ (Rom. 8:29).

There is no doubt about the believer's hope. It is not wishful thinking, but certainty. The reason the believer may be sure of his hope is that the Holy Spirit has been given to him as the down payment for the future realization of it. God has given to the Christian "the earnest of the Spirit" (II Cor. 5:5). That word "earnest" means "first installment," something like an engagement ring. The Holy Spirit is the guarantee in the believer that someday he will receive his inheritance.

A proper understanding of the Holy Spirit is crucial to understanding the believer's place in the body. He indwells the believer, places him in the body, and is the guarantee of the future. All believers share in the same work of the Holy Spirit, so He is the author of the body's unity and the security of its hope.

One Lord. Every Christian confesses and serves the same Lord Jesus Christ. Jesus Christ is the same Lord of all members of His body, no matter what part of the world they are in, or even if they are dead or alive. Christians have a common Master, a common commitment and allegiance.

Strange, then, that sometimes they seem to be following different orders. The body was not made to function that way. I remember one day at home when I told my daughter, "Marcy, go and close the door."

Just as she started that way, my wife called, "Marcy, why are you closing the door? Leave it open!" Marcy was the victim of conflicting orders.

In the body, only Christ gives the orders. If Christians are in conflict, it's because some of them are confusing the orders from the head. They are out of touch, mistaking their own desires, perhaps, for the will of Christ. Each part of the body needs to be in close, daily touch with the head, so that His directions are not confused.

Common fidelity to one Lord is a recurring theme in the New Testament. Speaking to the Gentiles in the home of Cornelius, Peter declared, "God is no respecter of persons. . . . The word which God sent unto the children of Israel, preaching peace by Jesus Christ: (he is Lord of all)" (Acts 10:34, 36). In that parenthetical remark Peter assured the Gentiles that Jesus is one Lord.

Notice also Romans 10:12:

> For there is no difference between the Jew and the Greek: for the same Lord over all is rich unto all that call upon him.

And again in I Corinthians 8:6:

> But to us there is but one God, the Father, of whom are all things, and we in him; and one Lord Jesus Christ. . . .

One faith. There are two possible interpretations here. The "one faith" may refer to the believer's exercise of saving faith, or it may refer to the content of the Gospel itself, the basic body of Christian truth.

In the first instance, the point would be that the believer comes to the one Lord by faith. The body includes no people who come other than by faith. In New Testament times the dispute was between Jew and Gentile. Are there two faith experiences or one? Paul answers, "Seeing it is one God, which shall justify the circumcision [the Jews] by faith, and uncircumcision [Gentiles] through faith" (Rom. 3:30).

There is no difference. Every believer comes into the body by faith alone. All Christians share a common means of salvation; they all come to Jesus Christ in faith.

However, there is ample evidence for holding the second view. Jude appeals to believers "to earnestly contend for the faith" (v. 3). He tells them to build themselves up "on your most holy faith" (v. 20). Paul affirms the same in Colossians 2:7: "Rooted and built up in him, and established in the faith."

In these cases "faith" is a body of truth, not the believer's response. The doctrines of the Gospel are what Christians believe in. They are objective facts, the truth of God's revelation to man. In this sense there is only "one faith." One leads to God. The Bible is one body of truth. Different parts of Christendom may offer different interpretations of the Truth, but there is basically one faith, one body of truth. Too often the body is rent by arguments over specifics. We must remember that there is not a Calvinistic New Testament and an Arminian New Testament, not a Baptist New Testament and a Presbyterian New Testament. The body of Christ holds to one faith.

Therefore, each member is responsible to dig into this one faith, to study it faithfully, diligently, with time and energy. "Study to shew thyself approved unto God, a workman that needeth not to be ashamed, rightly dividing the word of truth," Paul counseled Timothy (II Tim. 2:15). Each believer may become convinced of what the "one faith" teaches, but Scripture says he is to hold the truth in love. A fellow member of the body may not see a particular teaching in the same light; forbearance is necessary, not arrogant dogmatism. The body needs prayerful interaction, so that each member may be a corrective to the other. "One faith" can be expressed simply, clearly, and accurately—that should be our goal in the body.

One baptism. Bible scholars have two opinions

about this. Is this the baptism of the Holy Spirit, or the ordinance of water baptism? Since Spirit baptism is included in the concept of "one body, and one Spirit" (v. 4), it seems to me that "one baptism" refers to the ordinance.

There's a progression in verse 5. The body comprises those who have placed their faith in one Lord. What follows this expression of faith, according to New Testament practice? The ordinance of baptism. Having confessed faith in the Lord Jesus Christ, a person was baptized. The rite of baptism itself did not save the person, but it was a sign that he had committed himself to Christ.

Baptism is a matter of obedience to the Lord, along with observance of the Lord's Supper. The Great Commission given to the disciples by Jesus included baptism (Matt. 28:19). The early Christians followed this command. Wherever there was a confession of faith in Christ, there was a public baptism. Believers gave public testimony to their faith that way.

There was no hesitancy about it. The normal pattern was repentance, confession of faith, baptism, acceptance into the local church. Baptism was just one event in the regular pattern of things.

Paul's point of "one baptism" obviously was meant to stress the oneness of Jew and Gentile. No matter what your origin, when you came to Christ there was one baptism, not different baptisms according to your background. The Jews, of course, had practiced distinctive ceremonial washings, and they baptized proselytes. But in the new economy of the Gospel there were to be no distinctive baptisms, only one.

Therefore, it is just as essential to obey Christ in baptism as in anything else. It is not an option. It signifies the believer's own identification with the death, burial, and resurrection of Jesus. Water baptism symbolizes the end of the old life and the beginning of the new life. It is a sign to the world of what has transpired in the believer. Consequently, I believe it is only for adult believers, not for infants. Baptism follows faith; it doesn't save. It is an outward sign of an inner work of the Holy Spirit.

One God and Father of all. The work of the Trinity is revealed in this passage, for in a sense verse 4 is the Holy Spirit's verse, verse 5 the Son's verse, and verse 6 God the Father's verse. Here we have the climax, showing the total unity that is the reason for the believer's worthy walk. "One God," Paul says—the Sovereign of the Universe. He is "above all, and through all, and in you all." He upholds everything. He sustains and guides the world. What a source of assurance this is to the believer—God is in control!

However, He also expresses His loving and wise control in the believer. He is "in you all," that is, in everyone who has trusted in Christ, every member of the body. The God of the universe is the God of the individual. The Bible says not even a sparrow falls without His notice. He cares about the seemingly insignificant things.

"Know ye not that ye are the temple of God?" Paul asked (I Cor. 3:16). We are God-created, God-loved, God-controlled, God-sustained, and God-filled. Believers enjoy the peace and the power that result from having the very life of God in them.

This is the God of the seven-fold unity. God has done everything according to oneness. He wants the body to display that oneness, even as it is displayed in the Trinity. Everything God planned is one; therefore, it is reasonable that His one body should act accordingly. Unity is the essence of both the believer's high position and his lowly walk.

KINDS OF PERFECTION

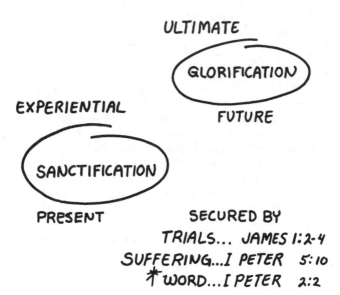

POSITIONAL

SALVATION

PAST

ULTIMATE

GLORIFICATION

FUTURE

EXPERIENTIAL

SANCTIFICATION

PRESENT

SECURED BY
TRIALS... JAMES 1:2-4
SUFFERING...I PETER 5:10
✝WORD...I PETER 2:2

There are three kinds of perfection: positional, accomplished by salvation in the past; ultimate, accomplished by glorification in the future; and experiential, accomplished by sanctification in the present. It is secured by trials, suffering, and, primarily, the Word.

Chapter Seven

PERFECTING THE BODY

In the Sermon on the Mount, Jesus made a shocking statement: "Be ye therefore perfect, even as your Father which is in heaven is perfect" (Matt. 5:48). Let's face it: that puts the standard pretty high, yet the same sentence tells us what the will of God is for all men who know Christ as personal Lord and Savior.

God's call is for His redeemed people to become perfect. The perfection of the body has been in the redemptive plan of God from eternity past. Throughout history God works to carry out this plan.

When we speak of perfecting the body, however, we must keep in mind that perfection is used three ways in Scripture. First, there is "positional perfection." When a person receives Jesus Christ, he becomes perfect positionally. Paul said, "We speak wisdom among them that are perfect" (I Cor. 2:6). He told the Colossian believers, "Ye are complete in him [Christ]" (2:10). The epistle to the Hebrews holds the same truth: "For the law made nothing perfect, but the bringing in of a better hope did" (7:19). That "better hope" was Christ. Also, "For by one offering he hath perfected forever them that are sanctified" (Heb. 10:14; cf. I Cor. 6:9-11).

Christ made redeemed men perfect. At the point of his salvation, the believer receives a positional perfection. His sin is removed and by position he becomes perfect before God, receiving Christ's righteousness as his own. Therefore, when he dies he may immediately enter God's presence.

The second kind is "ultimate perfection." Hebrews 12:23 mentions "the spirits of just men made perfect." John writes, "But we know that, when he shall appear, we shall be like him [Christ]; for we shall see him as he is" (I John 3:2). When the believer goes to be with God, he attains ultimate perfection. Paul has this end in mind when he confesses, "Not as though I had already attained, either were already perfect" (Phil. 3:12). He anticipates attaining "the resurrection of the dead" so that he might achieve ultimate perfection.

Between positional and ultimate perfection is "experiential perfection." Positionally and ultimately believers are perfect, but in experience they are far less. Christ's death and resurrection provided for the Christian's positional and ultimate perfection; His life in the believer provides for experiential perfection.

The whole point of the Christian life is to become experientially perfect. Believers are to grow, to mature, to attain practical Christian completeness. Note the phrase in Ephesians 4:12: "For the perfecting of the saints." That refers to experiential perfection of the body, not to either positional or ultimate perfection. The idea of experiential perfection is seen in the phrases, "unto a perfect man" (4:13); "be no more children" (v. 14); "grow up into him" (v. 15). The Christian is to attain "the measure of the stature of the fulness of Christ" (v. 13). The believer cannot attain sinlessness, but it is possible for him not to continually sin. He can become a well-rounded, grown-up believer. That is the concern of every member of the body: to be robust, vigorous, strong, vibrant. Babes in Christ are to grow up: experiential perfection.

The Greek word translated "perfecting" is from *katartismos*, which means "to equip something fully." It means something totally complete in itself, full-grown, filled to capacity. No Christian may settle to be less than fully equipped, mature, complete, grown-up, vigorous. The Apostle Paul urges in II Corinthians 7:1:

> Having therefore these promises, dearly beloved, let us cleanse ourselves from all filthiness of the flesh and spirit, perfecting holiness in the fear of God.

The whole body of Christ must be brought to full maturity.

The implication of Galatians 3:3 is that the believer is "made perfect" by the Holy Spirit. The Spirit uses trials and suffering to bring this about (James 1:2-4; I Pet. 5:10). He also uses the Word of God (I Pet. 2:2; II Tim. 3:16, 17). The Spirit's work is the benediction of Hebrews 13:20, 21:

> Now the God of peace, that brought again from the dead our Lord Jesus, that great shepherd of the sheep, through the blood of the everlasting covenant, Make you perfect in every good work to do his will. . . .

The most heartbreaking thing in my ministry is not that some people don't respond to the Gospel. It isn't that more people don't go to the mission field. The thing that breaks my heart most is that some members of the body remain spiritual babies all their lives; they never grow one inch from the time of their conversion. This is a denial of everything that God purposes for each member of the body.

God's plan to bring believers to maturity includes, with the work of the Holy Spirit, human instruments, also. Paul indicates this in Ephesians 4:11:

> And he gave some, apostles; and some, prophets; and
> some, evangelists; and some, pastors and teachers.

Why did God do this? "For the perfecting of the
saints." "Saints" are believers, all members of the
body. I'm here to perfect the saints. God gave the
early church apostles and prophets to perfect the
saints. He gives evangelists to perfect the saints.

Apostles, prophets, evangelists, pastor-teachers—all
are gifted men given to the body of Christ so that
Christians might be brought to perfection. We will
examine the character of each office in the next chapter of this book. Here we simply want to note God's
basic plan. These men are the agents of change in
the life of the church; they provide the dynamic
energy for spiritual growth; they are catalysts for
experiential perfection. The result of their ministry
is the body built up in love (Eph. 4:16).

In this passage (Eph. 4:11-16) we note three features of experiential perfection. (1) the progress to
perfection; (2) its purposes; (3) its power.

1. *The progress to perfection.* Paul outlines specific
steps in the body's maturing process. First, gifted
men equip the saints (vv. 11, 12a). The Lord Jesus
Christ won gifted men at the cross and gave them to
the church so that His children might be perfectly
equipped and mature in their faith.

These gifted men have specific ministries to this
end. Spiritual gifts for believers *en masse* are not in
view here, but for the men whom God has appointed
as leaders among the total body. Their ministries are
listed chronologically according to God's plan for the
development of the church.

Apostles. The apostles were a small group, orig-
inally appointed by Jesus Himself. They stood in
unique relation to the incarnate Lord: His constant
companions, witnesses to what He said and did,
"sent ones" to preach, heal, and cast out demons.
After the defection of Judas, Matthias was chosen to

take his place. To the Twelve Jesus gave the Great Commission. They were to become the authoritative source of the truth about Christ, as John explained:

That which was from the beginning, which we have heard, which we have seen with our eyes, which we have looked upon, and our hands have handled... declare we unto you (I John 1:1, 3).

Besides the Twelve, one other man belonged to the New Testament apostles. Because Jesus revealed Himself directly and spoke to him, Paul rightfully claimed apostleship (Eph. 1:1; Col. 1:1; Gal. 1:1). His unique call and commission formed the basis of his authority in the churches (see Acts 9).

Other men would fall into a secondary group of apostles: Barnabas, Silas, Timothy, and lesser known men like Andronicus and Junia (Rom. 16:7). They were apostles of the church, but not directly commissioned by the risen Lord.

Apostles had a specific purpose in God's plan. The church was "built upon the foundation of the apostles and prophets" (Eph. 2:20). Among other things, the mystery of the church was revealed through the "holy apostles and prophets by the Spirit" (Eph. 3:5). The apostles preached the original, basic truth that became the foundation of Christian doctrine. The early church subsisted on "the apostles' doctrine" (Acts 2:42). The gifted men affirmed God's truth authoritatively, based on the Old Testament Scriptures and what they had witnessed of Christ's teachings, death, and resurrection.

God confirmed apostolic authority by giving the ability to perform miracles. God authenticated their teaching "with signs and wonders, and with diverse miracles" (Heb. 2:4).

In the history of the early church, as recorded in Acts, the last time the apostles met as a body was at the Council of Jerusalem. After that they disappear from the written historical records, except for Paul and his fellowlaborers. As the Gospel spread and churches were founded, leadership fell to faithful men who followed the apostolic teaching. The apostles laid the foundation and brought the church to birth, so to speak. They planted churches and taught new believers in the Faith. But gradually local elders supplanted them. The tiny assemblies began to operate for themselves. As the building grew, the foundation was no longer in sight. So, the apostles as such were a temporary group of men, not a permanent fixture in the church. No one today may claim to be a New Testament apostle.

Prophets. Paul does not refer in Ephesians to Old Testament prophets but to New Testament ones, another temporary group of gifted men given to the infant church. Linked with the apostles (Eph. 2:20; 3:5), these men were needed as God's spokesmen. The New Testament did not exist. These prophets spoke directly from God, as did the Old Testament prophets.

Of course, this could lead to a problem, if a prophet began to give forth as authoritative something that was his own idea. For this reason Paul ordered that "the spirits of the prophets are subject to the prophets" (I Cor. 14:32). These men were to check on each other during the course of their ministry (14:29).

Prophetic ministry ceased with the writing of the New Testament. God doesn't speak to the church by direct revelation to individuals today. His "direct revelation" is in the words of Scripture, inspired by the Holy Spirit, inerrant and authoritative for the believer. The foundational ministry of apostles and prophets is past and no longer needed. God's revelation in the Bible is complete, emphatically warning against adding to it or subtracting from it (Rev. 22:18, 19). Believers need not seek direct prophetic revelation today; they need to know the Bible.

Evangelists. The New Testament picture of an

evangelist is of a man who goes from place to place where the Gospel has not been preached. He preaches Christ, leads people to faith in Him, and starts a little group of believers. He teaches them basic doctrine, appoints elders, and moves on to the next place; he is basically a planter of churches. The New Testament evangelist is not a person who comes to town for a week of meetings and then leaves. His work isn't finished until he has founded a church. Timothy and Philip are examples.

Pastor-teachers. The office declared here is one, not two. The idea is a teaching shepherd. He stays in one place, teaching the Gospel and sound doctrine, while at the same time pastoring the sheep. He takes over when the evangelist leaves.

The teaching shepherd's main task is to protect the flock. That's what shepherding is—protecting from both dangerous places and enemies. The pastor-teacher does this by building safeguards, teaching the truth, and helping those who may be stumbling into sin. He not only preserves them, but strengthens and encourages them. Jesus, of course, is the Great Shepherd. He loves His flock. He builds His church. He does so by giving the body gifted men—evangelists and pastor-teachers.

The body needs to recognize God's plan. In some churches leadership is in effect removed from the gifted men in the name of spiritual spontaneity and freedom of the Spirit. It is a serious error to think, "We'll just get together and see how the Spirit leads."

In God's plan for the body, the Holy Spirit does not have the responsibility for church order or planning services. In fact, at Corinth in the early church, a problem developed because of an apparent failure on the part of the ruling gifted men. There may have been some, but no elders are mentioned at Corinth. The believers tried to do their own thing, and this reaped chaos and confusion. So Paul rebuked them (I Cor. 14:23, 24) and reminded them that God is not

117

the author of confusion. Order is the responsibility of the gifted men whom God gives to the church. Whenever local church order is set loose, without careful guidance of Spirit-led, gifted men, the chances are great that some people will participate who are not Spirit-led. What occurs may be more sociological and psychological than biblical. The results are uncertain, confusing, and perhaps even demonic.

Thus apostles and prophets have been replaced in the body by church planters and teaching shepherds today. But the task now is the same as that of the original apostles and prophets: bring the believers to perfection. My work does not cease anywhere short of maturity in the lives of my flock. My ministry will not be complete so long as there is someone in my church who is not mature. My task is not to fill the building, but to equip the saints.

This passion for maturity in the body stands out in the New Testament writers. Note, for example, Paul's statement in Colossians 1:28:

Whom we preach [Christ], warning every man, and teaching every man in all wisdom; that we may present every man *perfect* in Christ Jesus.

Paul would settle for nothing less than maturity.

Then there was Epaphras, "a servant of Christ, . . . always laboring fervently for you in prayers, that ye may stand *perfect* and *complete* in all the will of God" (Col. 4:12, italics added). Epaphras is not famous like Paul, but he prayed passionately that every member of the body would reach maturity. This is always to be the passion of gifted men. The call to the ministry is not a call to a profession; it's a passion. God gives gifted men to the church, not to entertain it, program it, or organize it, but to bring believers to maturity. Nothing less satisfies the man of God (cf. James 1:4; Heb. 13:20, 21).

The question is, of course, "How does the man of God 'perfect the saints'?" How is this done in the local church today? The answer lies in three words: "Preach the word" (II Tim. 4:2). "Be instant [diligent] in season, out of season; reprove, rebuke, exhort with all long-suffering and doctrine." Preach the word! Hosea said, "My people are destroyed for lack of knowledge" (Hos. 4:6). The Word of God must be taught, to renew the mind, before life can become perfect (cf. Rom. 12:2; Eph. 4:23). Paul tells us in Colossians 1:28 that teaching perfects, and thus he is totally committed to it.

Paul expressed this command to Timothy in different ways.

> If thou put the brethren in remembrance of these things, thou shalt be a good minister of Jesus Christ, nourished up in the words of faith and of good doctrine. (I Tim. 4:6.)

Timothy's job was to transmit the things he learned to faithful men who in turn could teach others (II Tim. 2:2).

This pattern works in the ministry today. It is still God's plan: teach men who will teach others, who will in turn teach others, and so on. Teach what? The Word of God. Experiential perfection of the members of the body develops through the Word of God.

> All scripture is given by inspiration of God, and is profitable for doctrine, for reproof, for correction, for instruction in righteousness: That the man of God may be perfect, throughly furnished unto all good works (II Tim. 3:16, 17).

Scripture perfects!

Of course, the pastor-teacher himself must be a "workman" in the Word. He cannot teach it unless he studies it. This is part of his primary responsibility: study and teach the Word. The Word of God taught by men of God brings growth in the people of God.

That basic directive, "perfecting the saints," is the heart of the pastor's ministry. Anything less is a caricature. Spending time on other things is to miss God's basic calling. The pastor's heart should throb with the plea of Paul: "Night and day praying exceedingly that we might see your face, and might perfect that which is lacking in your faith" (I Thess. 3:10).

One of the tenderest scenes in all the Bible took place the day Paul left Ephesus, after three years of "perfecting the saints" there. The event is recorded in Acts 20:17-38. Every evangelist and teaching pastor should prayerfully study it. In it Paul characterizes his ministry in simple terms:

> I . . . have *taught* you publicly, and from house to house. . . . I have not shunned to declare unto you *all the counsel* of God (vv. 20, 27, italics added).

Paul had systematically taught the Ephesians Bible doctrine. Now he was leaving the same responsibility to the elders, the teaching pastors who would remain (v. 28). He sets forth the reasons for this commission: (1) the value of the church to God (v. 28b); (2) the inevitability of false teachers moving in with perverse dogma (vv. 29, 30); (3) the inabilty of anything else to build up the saints to maturity (v. 32).

The final words of the farewell speak in the most beautiful way of how believers will respond if the man of God properly teaches them: "And when he had thus spoken, he kneeled down, and prayed with them all. And they all wept sore, and fell on Paul's neck, and kissed him, Sorrowing most of all for the words which he spake" (vv. 36-38).

It was his "words"—the instruction in doctrine— that endeared him most to them. The people of God need the Word of God, and when it is given and bears fruit in their lives, their gratitude is a sweet reward.

The second stage in the progress to perfection is what believers themselves do. Note this in Ephesians 4:12: "For the perfecting of the saints for the work of the ministry . . ." Why do gifted men equip the saints? So that they might do the work of the ministry. The gifted men are to teach the Word to equip the saints to do the work. Teaching is the pastor's job.

Too often, however, this biblical pattern is thwarted by church members who expect pastors to do everything. No wonder some pastors suffer so much physical and emotional fatigue. Some have been driven to breakdowns—they can't find the time to study the Word of God—because their church members expect them not only to equip the saints, but to do the work of the ministry also. That is not God's plan for the body.

His plan is well illustrated by an incident in the early church. A dispute arose because certain widows were being neglected in the daily dispensing of food. The apostles resolved the matter with a significant decision. They told the church to appoint seven Spirit-filled men to look after the distribution of food, because "we will give ourselves continually to prayer, and to the ministry of the word" (Acts 6:4).

The apostles were not being proud or lazy. They were not above menial work. They were not above visiting people. But they were establishing a priority for their own ministry. They saw that their distinct contribution to the body was not menial activity, but praying and teaching the Word to equip the saints for the ministry. They rigidly adhered to the reason why God gave gifted men to the church.

The apostles also recognized that the body needs all members. There was a "work of the ministry" for each to perform. In fact, these parallel ministries of the gifted men and the members of the body show that the modern functional split between clergy and laymen is a false one. It destroys the beauty of the body. The gifted men given to the church are no better than the individual members; in God's plan He simply chose some to have the privilege of preaching and teaching. Having that role in the plan of God

121

does not elevate them qualitatively, just as it doesn't require them to be looking after a host of details unrelated to their primary calling. The dynamic of the early church came from a proper understanding of roles in the body: gifted men building up the saints, who in turn exercise spiritual ministries throughout the body.

Here we need to define "the work of the ministry for the edifying of the body" that the believers are called upon to perform. There are many church activities that cannot legitimately be called spiritual ministries, even though they are useful to the church program. This is not to minimize any activity—even putting up posters, for that matter—but it is to emphasize that the publicity chairman should also have a personal, spiritual ministry in the body.

God has given each member certain spiritual gifts (to be discussed in Chapter 8) for the work of the ministry. These spiritual gifts can be exercised in many ways: visiting the sick and shut-ins, counseling new Christians, praying and studying the Bible with others, taking food, clothes, and money to people in special need, showing personal love and care for the lonely and discouraged, reaching out to neighbors and friends with the Gospel.

The local church essentially is a training place to equip Christians to carry out their own ministries. Unfortunately, for many Christians the church is a place to go to watch professionals perform and to pay the professionals to carry out the church program. In many quarters Christianity has deteriorated into professional "pulpitism," financed by lay spectators. The church hires a staff of ministers to do all the Christian service.

This scheme is not only a violation of God's plan, but an absolute detriment to the growth of the church and the vitality of the members of the body. Every member needs to find a significant place of service. To limit the work of the ministry to a small, select class of full-time clergymen hinders the spiritual growth of God's people, stunts the development of the body, and hinders the evangelistic outreach of the church into the community.

From the members who give themselves to the work of the ministry God Himself will choose certain ones to be His gifts to the church as a whole. This is a never-ending cycle. Every congregation ought to be producing faithful workers, some of whom in turn will be called by God to become full-time evangelists and pastor-teachers. This is exactly what happened in Philip's life. His ministry began as a Spirit-filled deacon (Acts 6:5), and then God called him to a wide evangelistic ministry (Acts 8:5-40). Those called by God will then be used by Him to train others, and from those thus trained God will in turn call more gifted ones. This is basic to His plan for the perfection of the body.

I am more and more committed to the proposition that each local church ought to be developing its own spiritual leadership. Instead of bringing in outside men to fill these positions, the church ought to rear its own people to spiritual maturity. If a church is not producing competent leaders to serve Christ in a full-time capacity, something is wrong.

At Grace Community Church our dozen or so gifted men and staff leaders have all come from within the ranks of the congregation. God has brought them to maturity by His Spirit, through His Word. These people were "faithful in a little," so to speak, and then God gave them a larger responsibility. The result for our church has been a unique quality of unity, fellowship, and commitment to each other—leaders and flock alike—which is more difficult to achieve if the ministering staff is assembled from outside the congregation. The first level of my ministry has been to "disciple" these people. Our staff has grown from the soil of much time that I have given

123

to each one in personal fellowship, teaching, and prayer.

In fact, though I pray and work for souls to be saved, I have never deliberately sought more people to swell our numbers. I have no right to ask God for more people until I see some progress in those He has already given me to equip. Thank God, there has been progress. We see the saints feeding and loving each other, counseling each other, caring for each other, nourishing each other, and even developing, organizing, and operating various ministries within the church.

I remember seeing, at a circus, a man spinning plates on eight sticks. He would just get all eight going and have to run back to keep Number One moving, and so on up the line. This seems to me an apt illustration of the role of the pastor, who has figured out the plates he wants to spin and looks through the congregation to find the right sticks. He gets it all going and discovers that the sticks don't keep the plates moving, so he is stuck with running up and down from plate to plate, operating programs which the sticks are not motivated to spin. How much better is it to concentrate all on "perfecting the sticks" so that as they grow they become motivated to begin certain ministries, services that are on their hearts and interest them. Perfected, mature saints will develop ministries in the energy and excitement of their maturity.

The result: the body of Christ is edified (Ephesians 4:12). The whole body comes together. When each member does his own work of the ministry, the whole body comes to maturity.

When the body is built up, more people are won to Christ. A strong, unified, loving, serving body has a dynamic testimony to the world. For the body to be built up, every part must be involved—gifted men "perfecting the saints," and the saints doing the work of the ministry. That is the progress of perfection.

2. *The purpose of perfection.* What are the results of experiential perfection? Five are specified by Paul in Ephesians 4:13-15.

Unity of the faith. If gifted men equip the saints, and the saints do the work of the ministry, the body grows and believers are united. The body that is mature and working and serving will be united. If sometimes there is breakdown, it is because either the pastor doesn't teach the word to equip the believers, or the believers do not accept their responsibility of ministry.

Because the whole body is affected, it disturbs me to see pastors and evangelists who are not perfecting believers by teaching the Word. They have active programs, but their schedules are so busy that they do not study the Word and teach it in every service. One pastor friend simply cannot believe that I teach the Bible at every service.

Our biblical pattern is Acts 2:42:

> They continued stedfastly in the apostles' doctrine and fellowship, and in breaking of bread, and in prayers.

This produced the unity of the body in Acts 4:32:

> The multitude of them that believed were of one heart and of one soul; neither said any of them that aught [any] of the things which he possessed was his own; but they had all things common.

These believers also had great boldness and power in their witness to Christ. They won people to Him every day (Acts 2:47).

Because they gave themselves to the study of the Word and ministered to each other, their love and unity had a profound impact on the world. If the body is to be one, it cannot break down at any point.

Knowledge of the Son of God. When the believer follows God's purpose for perfection, he comes to a deep, deep knowledge of Jesus Christ. This deep knowledge follows his growth in understanding the

Word of God, his growth in maturity, his growth in personal ministry, and his growth in oneness. Some Christians' knowledge of Christ is limited to His saving work on their behalf. In God's purpose for perfecting the saints, however, the believer is to grow in more intimate fellowship with Christ. The body that is learning and serving will be deeply involved with Jesus Christ. The maturing Christian experiences a richer and richer personal fellowship with the Son of God.

The measure of the stature of the fullness of Christ. As the body is progressively perfected according to God's purposes, it becomes more and more like Jesus Christ. That's the result of the deeper, more intimate fellowhip with Him.

Paul describes the believer's goal: "unto a perfect man." The word implies a fully developed, robust, strong, mature person. God is not satisfied when we accept anything less for our standard. The perfect man, of course, is Christ; to measure how mature you are, how perfect, you must compare yourself with Him. No one has arrived spiritually until he attains His stature. Once in a while a person thinks he has made a great spiritual stride, but lest he think there's no further to go, Paul keeps the standard before him: "the fullness of Christ."

God's plan for moving toward that fullness is plain: teach the Word, equip the saints for the work of ministry, unity in the body, a deeper knowledge of Christ. Each believer finds himself involved somewhere in this process of spiritual growth and development. He keeps moving toward the goal: be as perfect as Jesus was. Jesus shows the Christian what God's perfection is and then says, "Be like Me."

It's easy, of course, to stop off at some lower level, but the progressively perfected believer will settle for nothing less than the fullness of Christ. He will constantly strive to be like Jesus in everything he does, not just so he can say that he has achieved something, but because he wants to show his love for Christ. Love is the motive. I want to be like Jesus because I love Him.

One day I asked my son, Mark, what he wanted to be when he grew up. "I'm going to be a dad, just like you," he said. "Well, why do you want to be a dad just like me?" I asked him. "Because I love you," he said. He wanted to be like me because he loves me. Since I am the object of his love as his father, he wants to emulate me. I am the nearest standard he has.

If Christians really love Jesus, they will want to be like Him. If they don't care enough to try to be like Him, perhaps their profession of love for Him is a sham.

Solid in doctrine.

> That we henceforth be no more children, tossed to and fro, and carried about with every wind of doctrine, by the sleight of men, and cunning craftiness, whereby they lie in wait to deceive (Eph. 4:14).

Children are gullible and undiscerning. They don't know what's good or bad. Give them a choice of diet, and they'll get sick. Children will believe anyone. God's purpose in perfecting His children is that in the spiritual realm they will not act like gullible, undiscerning children when it comes to doctrine. They are not to be susceptible to every new religious fad. They are to be strong, firm, confident of what they believe—not tossed about by the shifting winds of ungodly philosophies.

Some Christians, because they are spiritual babies, fall victim to false teaching. But if a believer follows God's plan for perfection, is well taught, and gives himself to spiritual ministry, he is not going to be swayed by error. Rather than being thrown off by it, he will be able to expose it. God's will is for every believer to grow up out of spiritual childhood and so not be in an exposed position when "crafty" deceivers come around.

In I John 2:13, 14, John speaks of levels of spiritual growth. The second level, "young men," are those who conquer Satan. Since Satan's major effort is in false doctrine, it indicates that only those who have grown from babies to young men spiritually can deal with the problem.

Evangelism. "Speaking the truth in love . . ." (Eph. 4:15). This is the last purpose of perfection of the body. The climax is the proclamation of God's truth, in love, by every believer, both to other believers and to the unbeliever. This is the end result for the Christian who really knows Christ, who wants to be like Him, who is strong in faith and doctrine. Proclaiming the truth is the believer's work of the ministry, something he himself can do in his community and at work.

God's plan of perfection for the body is progressive. He gives gifted men to the church to equip the saints. The saints thus equipped do the work of the ministry. The body grows and is built up. The body comes together in unity. Individual members have a deep, abiding fellowship with Christ. They grow in Christ-likeness; they know sound doctrine, combat false teaching, and go into the community with a dynamic, loving presentation of the Gospel.

3. *The power of perfection.* In discussing the perfection of the believer in the body, it is easy to get the impression that everything depends on us. True, Scripture clearly outlines human responsibility—gifted men are to teach, the saints are to respond and grow. But if that were the end of the matter it would be just another humanistic scheme. Thus perfection is not achieved by human strength. Notice the connection between Ephesians 4:15 and 16:

> . . . Christ: From whom the whole body fitly joined together and compacted by that which every joint supplieth, according to the effectual working in the

128

measure of every part, maketh increase of the body unto the edifying of itself in love.

The body will grow up as every part works. As every member serves, the body will mature to perfection. But how does the body grow? Better, from whom does it grow? Jesus Christ.

Ephesians 4:16 is a summation of verses 11-15. Verse 16 shows where the power comes from to make the progress and purposes of perfection actually happen. "Christ, from whom the whole thing happens." Without this statement, perfection appears to rest solely with the individual. But the power is really Jesus Christ's, working in and through the believer. Organizations and programs are not here, just a body ministering for spiritual purposes.

The power of Christ unto the perfection of the body will be unleashed when the Word of God is faithfully proclaimed and when the saints do the work of the ministry.

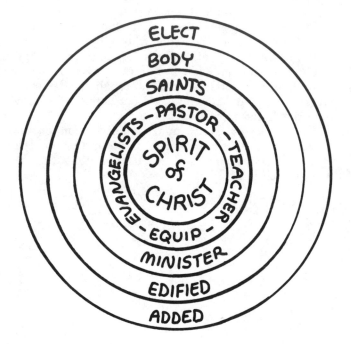

The pattern for the church begins with the power of the Spirit and extends through the progress to perfection until the elect are added.

Chapter Eight

THE GIFTS OF THE BODY

God wants to reach the whole world with His truth. Therefore, the Holy Spirit has specially empowered and enabled the members of the body to carry out some very important functions. In the Old Testament, Israel was God's vehicle to reach the world. In the New Testament era Jesus and His disciples were God's vehicles. Today the church, Christ's body, is the vehicle God uses to communicate to the world His nature and His truth.

The church's witness is not only verbal; it is not only a communication of the Gospel in specifics; it is the witness of love and unity. When believers are one in love, the world will find their witness impressive. A unity, built on humility and love, becomes the church's greatest testimony. But though believers are one in position, though they have been made one in terms of the Holy Spirit's ministry putting them into the body of Christ, though they are one in the Holy Spirit, they are not one in spirit. The world does not see them as one in practice. They do not have a singular testimony of humility and love.

If God wants Christians to be one, Satan wants them to be divided. So, while the prayer of Christ was that Christians would be one, and while the activity of the Holy Spirit is to make them one, all of the energy of Satan is to fracture Christian unity. Whenever a divisive issue arises within the body of Christ, we can be sure one side is the agent of Satan. Christ wants to unify; Satan wants to divide. There are so many carnal Christians that Satan can get away with all the division he wants. He has been tremendously successful.

There is no scriptural justification for all the present divisions of the church. There were no divisions denominationally in the New Testament. In fact, all church divisions are explicitly contrary to the teaching of the Word of God. The whole intent of Christ, in forming the body, was that believers may be one, not divided into little parts.

Was the body formed in discord or in unity? In unity, of course. In the Book of Acts, the body of Christ was formed in a prayer meeting in the upper room of a house in Jerusalem. The disciples of Jesus gathered there to pray. Out of their faith, obedience, and waiting in prayer, God brought into being the church. In that prayer gathering, the hour of another divine dispensation struck. Men and women filled with the Holy Spirit, and possessing gifts of the Holy Spirit, went out of the room into the streets to preach Christ crucified and risen and to announce God's free grace. They were humble people. There were no great ones, no mighty ones. They had no organizational structure; they just prayed and waited.

That was the birth of the church—of the body of Christ. It was accomplished in the energy of the Holy Spirit. Every member who was part of that prayer meeting was engaged in the activities through the Spirit's power. From that moment on, every member has been added to the church the same way —by the Spirit's power, placing him into the body of

Christ. Christians are as singularly one today as they were in Acts 2.

The church was exciting. Believers were all filled with the Spirit. They were all exercising their spiritual gifts. They were all preaching the Gospel. They had a unity of humble love that was manifest everywhere. The world was shaken. People couldn't believe what was happening in Jerusalem. Believers were added daily to the church.

In order for the church today to be an effective witness as a body, as the early church was, it must be as healthy as the early church was. Not just organized, but Spirit-filled. Not just super-committed, but exercising the spiritual gifts. Not just giving out publicity, but preaching the Gospel. The standards have not changed. Christians must be mature, functioning, loving, humble, Spirit-filled, exercising gifts, preaching the Gospel, just as the early church was.

Christ wants the church to be powerful; He wants the church to be mature; He wants the church to be functioning; He wants the church to be growing; He wants the church to be witnessing and manifesting His love. In order to accomplish this, God designed a plan for the church—not a church building or an organization. This is God's plan. Besides the gifted man given to the church (Eph. 4:11, 12), to make the church really grow, and have a unified witness, God designed every member to have a certain function, or functions, within the body. Since Christ wants a healthy body—growing, maturing, functioning, and witnessing—every member must have a ministry that lends itself to the health of that body. The human body is an illustration of this. It has all kinds of organs that interact, and all kinds of limbs that interact. If just one of your organs doesn't function, the whole body feels it. The same thing is true of the body of Christ; every organ has a function that affects the health of the whole body. Every believer has a necessary ministry as a vital organ of the body.

If the body is to be healthy and mature, and thus have a single dynamic testimony to the world, every believer must actively and intensely involve himself in the function God has given him. His services and ministry make the body healthy because he carries strength to the other vital parts. His failure to serve makes the body sick.

God's will for the body is that Christians be like Christ. In Ephesians 4:13 Paul says,

> Till we all come in the unity of the faith, and of the knowledge of the Son of God, unto a perfect man, unto the measure of the stature of the fulness of Christ.

The total body is to be like Jesus Christ. Through the church Christ wants to manifest His own character; He wants to manifest His person through believers, not only as individuals but as a body. To accomplish this, God gives every member a function that ministers to the rest of the body, certain spiritual gifts that each one has.

All the spiritual gifts are, in their fullest sense, complete in Christ. The gift of preaching. Did Christ preach with power in the Spirit? The gift of teaching; did He teach? Showing mercy; did He show mercy? Helps, ruling—no matter what the gift, it was complete in Christ. The reason God gives each member these different gifts is that He wants the body to manifest a composite Christlikeness. Every gift believers have was complete and perfect in Christ. He gives members of the body these various gifts that they might be built up to His own fullness. The gifts are not random; they are Christ's characteristics reproduced by the Spirit in the body. This means that the only way an individual Christian will ever be a man of full stature in Christ is when he has all those gifts being ministered to him. A Christian can never be completely like Jesus Christ until he has been built up in all the areas represented by the spiritual gifts.

134

That is one reason why each believer must minister his gift to another believer. As one ministers to another, he builds him up in that area. If I minister the gift of preaching, my people should learn from my ministering how to communicate more effectively. If a believer in my church has the gift of showing mercy, and he ministers that gift to me, I not only receive the direct blessing and purpose of that gift, but I learn a little more about how to show mercy. I may not have that gift, but in a lesser degree, I'm built up in that area. As each member ministers to the other, they are all built up as individuals to be like Christ and to show forth all His attributes. Collectively, as a body, they manifest the total person of Christ. This is not meant to imply that all believers should minister all gifts, nor that each Christian becomes a body by himself.

Spiritual gifts are what the New Testament calls "grace gifts" (charismata). The gifts are of grace; a Christian doesn't earn them. Nothing indicates that the more spiritual he gets, the more gifts he gets.

From I Corinthians 12 we will consider four features of spiritual grace gifts: (1) the importance of spiritual gifts; (2) their source; (3) their power; (4) their extent.

1. *The importance of spiritual gifts.* Why are they important? We have seen that the body can't be like Christ unless the gifts are ministered and Christians all grow together in maturity in all the areas that characterize Christ. How can I say I am like Christ if I don't know something of how to show mercy, or if I don't know at all how to teach? How can I know these things unless someone who has the gift ministers to me? Spiritual gifts are important because unless believers minister them in the energy of the Spirit, the body is not built up. And if it is not built up, it is not like Christ, I am not like Christ, and

Christians are not what they ought to be—a body to manifest Christ to the world.

The importance of spiritual gifts is seen in Paul's statement, "Now concerning spiritual gifts, brethren, I would not have you ignorant" (I Cor. 12:1). That very statement indicates how important this is. Unfortunately, some believers are ignorant: the Corinthian believers were grossly ignorant. Some people abuse the spiritual gifts; some neglect them. Some Christians emphasize only the sign gifts, the miraculous gifts, and ignore the edifying ones. It is essential for the ministry of the local church that Christians understand spiritual gifts. No local congregation will be what it should be, what Jesus prayed that it should be, what the Holy Spirit gifted it and empowered it to be, until it understands spiritual gifts.

2. *The source of spiritual gifts.*

But all these [Paul has just referred to the spiritual gifts] worketh that one and the selfsame Spirit, dividing to every man severally as he will (I Cor. 12:11).

What is the source of the spiritual gifts? The Holy Spirit. God gives these gifts through the Spirit; the Spirit takes the various gifts and distributes them to the body members. The day the Christian was born into the family of God, the day that he received Jesus Christ as his personal Savior, the Spirit of God distributed to him certain gifts.

A spiritual gift is a Spirit-given ability which acts as a channel through which the Holy Spirit ministers to the body. The spiritual gift is not the end in itself; it is only the channel through which the Holy Spirit operates. Every believer has spiritual gifts, regardless of his personal spiritual development, because possession of spiritual gifts doesn't mean a Christian is "spiritual." The only question is whether the channel is clear or plugged up. Many people think that when they have attained some spiritual gifts they are instantly spiritual. A spiritual gift never has anything to do with spirituality. One can have all of the gifts recorded in Scripture and still be an unspiritual man. This was true of some believers at Corinth (cf. I Cor. 1:7 with I Cor. 3:1-4).

Some people think they should seek certain gifts. They are told to "tarry" for certain gifts. Some even follow gimmicks and techniques to get them. They attempt to generate artificial, emotional, and even Satanic activity, and then call such activity the gifts of the Spirit. The Holy Spirit is the source of spiritual *gifts,* not self-induced hysteria, not Satanic counterfeits. The Holy Spirit gives the gifts by divine will and divine choice. He knows what gifts are needed, where they are needed, when they are needed, and who is to receive them.

It is also true that one can have a gift from the Holy Spirit and be doing nothing about it. Timothy is an example. Paul told him,

Neglect not the gift that is in thee (I Tim. 4:14).

Timothy had become sidetracked by certain people who were pressuring him. He was getting upset. He didn't lose his gift—he had it. He just neglected it. Later on evidently Timothy still wasn't doing too well.

Wherefore I put thee in remembrance that thou stir up the gift of God. (II Tim. 1:6.)

A spiritual gift is not the same as a natural ability. You can't say "My gift is making pie." That's a wonderful ability, but that is not a gift of the Spirit. Or some may say, "My gift is to work with my hands," or "My gift is to sing." Those are not spiritual gifts; those are natural abilities. The spiritual gifts are sovereignly bestowed manifestations of the Spirit's power.

The Apostle Paul illustrates the difference between a spiritual gift and a natural ability. He obviously

137

had natural ability to express himself publicly; but it is clear that he never regarded his ability to speak as a gift of the Spirit. He was also a man of tremendous learning. He could have used his knowledge of philosophy and literature to compose eloquent, convincing orations. He could have delivered them with magnificent ability. But he said this:

> And I, brethren, when I came to you, came not with excellency of speech or of wisdom, declaring unto you the testimony of God. For I determined not to know any thing among you, except Jesus Christ, and him crucified (I Cor. 2:1, 2).

The Holy Spirit expresses Himself through men. He uses a man's knowledge and ability, but in a supernatural way apart from man's own ability.

Many people have the gift of gab, and they aren't preachers. If a man has a natural aptitude along that line, perhaps the Holy Spirit will elect to use it; perhaps He won't. A gift of manifestation of the Spirit is of the Spirit, not of the flesh. If a Christian is really fluent in his speech, perhaps God will put him in a totally different area in the body of Christ than teaching or preaching. Perhaps he will be ministering in a way that isn't even visible publicly. And yet, he may have the ability to speak.

On the other hand, I recall a friend in seminary who had a severe stuttering problem. My first reaction when I heard him in speech class was "There is no way that he belongs in the ministry as a preacher." Today he is a preacher—and a fine Bible teacher. He is a good expositor of the Word of God, and a lucid speaker, even though he still struggles with words. He does not have a natural gift of eloquence, but he has the gift of the Spirit in that area.

So God may elect to use a Christian's natural ability, but He may give him a spiritual gift that has no connection with his natural ability. Relying upon natural ability for the production of spiritual fruit is a hindrance to what the Spirit wants to do. I Peter 4:10, 11 illustrates this:

> As every man hath received the gift, even so minister the same one to another, as good stewards of the manifold grace of God. If any man speak, let him speak as the oracles of God; if any man minister, let him do it as of the ability which God giveth, that God in all things may be glorified through Jesus Christ, to whom be praise and dominion for ever and ever.

There is a difference between the ability to speak and the Spirit-given gift of preaching.

On the other hand, it is possible for a man to have the gift of preaching, yet stand in the pulpit and preach in the flesh. I can verify, by personal experience, that it is a constant battle in my own heart and mind not to speak humanly, but as the oracle of God, to bring my gifts into subjection to the Holy Spirit.

The fact that one has a spiritual gift doesn't necessarily mean he always ministers it in the Holy Spirit. I Corinthians 14:32 says: "And the spirits of the prophets are subject to the prophets." That means that even one called to be a preacher (prophet) has to subject his spirit. I am not spiritual because I preach. I Corinthians 14:29 says: "Let the prophets speak two or three, and let the others judge." The prophets are fallible, so they must check each other to verify what they say. Spiritual gifts are no guarantee that a believer is always right.

In summary, we have seen that having a spiritual gift does not necessarily mean a Christian is spiritual. Gifts are given by the Holy Spirit, not necessarily in accordance with natural ability or disability. A believer can minister his gift in the energy of either the Spirit or the flesh.

3. *The power of spiritual gifts.* I Corinthians 12:2 says: "Ye know that ye were Gentiles, carried away unto these dumb idols, even as ye were led." The

word "led" refers to leading a prisoner. The unsaved person is seen in a kind of pathetic hopelessness, worshiping false gods who cannot speak because they do not exist. Verse 3 of the same chapter says,

Wherefore I give you to understand, that no man speaking by the Spirit of God calleth Jesus accursed: and that no man can say that Jesus is the Lord, but by the Holy Ghost.

A person can know nothing about Christianity and spiritual gifts if the Holy Spirit does not teach him. Even something as basic as the Lordship of Christ cannot be known unless the Holy Spirit reveals it. When Peter said to Jesus, "Thou art the Christ, the Son of the living God," Jesus replied, "Flesh and blood hath not revealed it unto thee, but my Father which is in heaven" (Matt. 16:16, 17).

To paraphrase Paul, "I don't want you to be ignorant about spiritual gifts, but I know this, you couldn't know about them, because you don't know the basics. You couldn't know about spiritual gifts, you couldn't know about step one—the Lordship of Christ—apart from the Holy Spirit." The flesh is incapable of knowing anything (cf. I Cor. 2:10). If the natural man can't even understand the Lordship of Christ, how can he understand the work of the Holy Spirit through spiritual gifts? Spiritual understanding and spiritual work can only be done by the power of the Spirit. Jesus said, "Ye shall receive power, after that the Holy Ghost is come upon you" (Acts 1:8). Who then is the power for understanding and for operating spiritual gifts? The Holy Spirit!

Whatever a Christian does on his own, in his own flesh, in his own fashion, in his own will and design, is a waste, failure, and mockery. But whatever he does when filled by the Holy Spirit, when using his gift by His power, is borne along by divine energy. A Christian doesn't have to build up his strength himself. He says, "Spirit of God, use me," and divine energy flows to the body as he ministers. The service of the body, every member's gift, must be exercised in the energy of the Holy Spirit if it is to be effective. The Corinthian believers had the gifts, but through carnality they had quenched and grieved the Holy Spirit. No power was coming through. The Corinthian part of the body was sick.

There are three steps to using one's gift in the energy of the Spirit. (1) Prayer. Constantly ask God to cleanse your life, to use you in the Spirit's power. (2) Yield yourself (cf. Rom. 6:16; 12:1, 2). (3) Be filled with the Holy Spirit (Eph. 5:18). Allow the Spirit of God to permeate every part of you. Turn every decision, every thought, every attitude over to the Spirit's control. Commitment to His control is the key.

4. *The extent of spiritual gifts.* By extent we mean: to what extent do believers have them, how many are there, and what are they? How many believers have the gifts? They all have them. They are channels given to every believer through which the Spirit manifests Himself to the body.

How many gifts are there? Some are listed in Romans 12:6-8 and some in I Corinthians 12:8-10, 28. There is no absolute reason to assume that these are all the gifts there are, but these certainly must be the key ones. They are here for our study, so we will make a composite of the two lists and consider each gift.

There are two kinds of spiritual gifts, permanent, edifying ones and temporary, confirming sign gifts.

a. Permanent gifts which edify or build up the body. These are gifts which do not cease, which began in the early church and still go on today.

The gift of prophecy. The gift of prophecy means preaching, not foretelling the future. It means "to tell forth, to declare." It is important to understand that there is a gift of prophecy and there is a gifted man called a prophet (see Chapter 7). The gift of prophecy is not to be confused with the office of prophet. I Corinthians 12:28 shows the difference. I Corinthians 12:10 says prophecy is a gift, but verse 28 says, "And God hath set some in the church, first apostles, secondarily prophets, thirdly teachers...." They are men, not gifts. "Some" doesn't refer to gifts, but to men. Paul continues, "... after that miracles, then gifts of healings, helps..." The gifts are distinguished by the little phrase "after that." God established certain men in the church, and on top of that He gave certain gifts. God has not only given every member of the body of Christ certain gifts, He's also given the church in total certain gifted men. The prophet and the gift of prophecy are thus distinct. The New Testament prophets belonged to a special group for a special time in history. They belonged to the first century church, the apostolic era. There are no prophets today anymore than there are apostles.

Though the prophets have ceased, the gift of prophecy, or preaching, still goes on. That's why Paul says "Follow after charity, and desire spiritual gifts, but rather that ye may prophesy" (I Cor. 14:1). The word "prophesy" means "preach." Preaching is defined by Paul's use of three words, "But he that prophesieth (preaches) speaketh unto men to edification, and exhortation, and comfort" (14:3). Preaching is building up, encouraging, and comforting. The best way to preach is given by Paul to Timothy in these words: "Till I come, give attendance to reading, to exhortation, to doctrine" (I Tim. 4:13). Paul advocates expository preaching here as he says, in effect, "Read the text, explain the text, apply the text." The implication is that much preaching only departs from the text. Comparing the gift of prophecy with tongues, Paul says, "He that speaketh in an unknown tongue edifieth himself, but he that prophesieth edifieth the church" (I Cor. 14:4). Preaching was a dominant ministry.

142

There are some efforts today to play down the centrality of preaching, but preaching is still a gift of the Spirit and it is to be sought in the ministry of the church. No service of the body is complete without a declaration of God's truth. The preaching of the Cross is still central in the gathering of the church. Some churches have only one preaching service a week—that is not putting prophecy in the exalted place it should have. It is primary because it edifies and builds the body. The standard of true preaching was whether or not the prophet's words squared with the words of Jesus Christ (I Cor. 14:37). The gift of preaching today is exercised under the same standard. The standard for preaching is not *Time* magazine, *Newsweek*, or politics. It's not someone's philosophy or a book review. It's the Word of God. Preaching *(kerygma)* always includes teaching *(didache)*.

Having the gift of preaching does not necessarily mean you have to exercise it in a formal sermon. The gift of preaching may be exercised to children, or to young people, or a class of adults. The gift of preaching is a Spirit-given and Spirit-energized ability to proclaim the truths of Jesus Christ. The setting or the size of the audience doesn't determine the gift. And although prophecy is a special gift given to some and only some, all Christians are to be preachers to some degree. All Christians are witnesses to Christ.

The gift of teaching. The gift of teaching is distinct from the teacher. There is a gift of teaching, and there is a gifted man, a teacher (cf. I Cor. 12:28). The office of teaching did not end; it still exists. God still appoints teachers. Only the apostles and prophets ended with the apostolic era. This was because they were the foundation of the church (Eph. 2:20; 3:5). The continuing ministries belong to teachers, teaching-pastors, and evangelists. Those are the three existing ministries that followed the foundational ministries of apostles and prophets. It's one thing to have the gift of teaching; it's another to be an appointed teacher. Teachers were appointed in the early church, and given specific positions to teach, even as now. Some of the great professors in evangelical seminaries, some of the great Bible teachers who travel the world—all are divinely appointed teachers, given to the church, and on top of that, they have the gift of teaching.

But any believer may have the gift of teaching and not be appointed to a teaching office in terms of a total ministry to the church. There are many body members who have not been called to a ranking position as teachers, but they have the gift of teaching. Basically, teaching is the ability to take a Christian and teach him the truths of the Word of God. It's not the same as preaching. It's one thing to declare and proclaim; it's something else to sit down with a new-born babe, put your arm around him, and instruct him in the things of God. That's the gift of teaching. It can be exercised in a Sunday school class; or in a home; or in a counseling situation. Of course, it's possible for a person to have both preaching and teaching gifts.

Teaching is a special gift, but every Christian is to be in some sense a teacher. Every believer's responsibility is to teach at some level: with fellow believers, with his own family, or in small groups of neighbors and friends (cf. Gal. 6:6; II Tim. 2:2, 15).

In the body teaching and preaching provide a balanced ministry: evangelism and edification. Preaching is motivating, teaching is instruction. They go side-by-side.

The gift of faith. Faith is one of the Spirit-given gifts. All believers have faith, but some have a special gift of faith. I believe this could just as well be called "the gift of prayer." It is not just faith in something for no reason. Faith moves the hand of God. Some Christians have a way of laying hold of God in faith in the special energy of the Spirit.

The gift of wisdom. This is the ability to see deeply

into the mysteries of God. It is the kind of insight that sees what the natural eye can't see; that hears what the natural ear cannot hear. It's the ability to take a simple phrase of Scripture, or a simple truth of God, and dive into it and pull out of it all the spiritual truth and mystery that's there. The gift of wisdom is the ability to take that truth and apply it to life. A simple definition of wisdom is "the application of spiritual truth." Dig it out and put it into practice. In a sense, all believers are to have wisdom (Col. 1:9; James 1:5), but some have the gift of wisdom. They rise above to minister to the body in a unique way.

The gift of knowledge. If wisdom is the application of truth, knowledge is just the facts and nothing more. Knowledge is understanding the facts, that's it; scholarship in a human sense. These are the scholars who dig into the Scripture. They research. Some spend all their lives studying ancient manuscripts, archeology, and all kinds of scholarly problems. They are able, by the Spirit of God, to search out the facts. Upon their work we build our faith. Our Bible didn't just drop out of heaven; it took years and years of labor to determine which manuscripts were right.

Knowledge is the academic side of truth; wisdom is application. Some Christians have both gifts. Some have neither, and some have one. None of these gifts operates according to human ability. Just because a man has an IQ of 165 doesn't mean he has the gift of knowledge or the gift of wisdom. Some of the wisest people I've met didn't have an IQ like that. But they had the Spirit-given gift of wisdom. These are spiritual gifts, not intellectual; they come about not by education but by a sovereign act of the Holy Spirit. A believer's insights into Scripture do not depend on his IQ.

Even though there's a gift of knowledge, all Christians are responsible to have knowledge. All are responsible to study to show themselves approved unto God. Both wisdom and knowledge are to belong to every believer (I Cor. 1:5, 30). And yet, even though we're all to have these spiritual qualities, there is a certain sense in which some Christians are specially gifted and rise above to minister to the body.

The discernment of spirits. God wanted to protect the church from false doctrine. So He gave certain members of the body the ability to determine who was right and who was wrong. Some believers have the ability to discern the spirits, that is, whether they are of God or of Satan. The body faces continual opposition from a host of demons who pose as messengers of light, trying to counterfeit the gifts of the Spirit and sap the energy of the church. Because of this, God gave certain gifts so that men could discern between God and Satan, something beyond natural insight.

Peter used this gift when he asked Ananias, "Why hath Satan filled thine heart to lie to the Holy Spirit?" (Acts 5:3). How did Peter know? He knew because he had the gift of discernment. Every Christian in a sense is to be discerning.

> Beloved, believe not every spirit, but try [test] the spirits whether they are of God: because many false prophets are gone out into the world (I John 4:1).

Every believer is to be sensitive to spirits, knowing whether they're of God or Satan.

The gift of showing mercy. Next we come to the *love gifts.* Although all the gifts are to be ministered in love, yet there are three distinct love gifts that minister to the body. The first one is the *gift of showing mercy.* Some people can't preach a sermon, but they can do deeds of loving kindness. This is Christ's love, manifested by the Holy Spirit, through the believers to the body. It's not just sympathy; it's not exercised out of duty. Some persons just have that gift of compassionate love that causes them to do things of kindness to others. Some of the greatest

146

testimony to Christ is given without a word being spoken; love is expressed without saying a thing.

Obviously, all believers are to show deeds of mercy.

> If a brother or sister be naked, and destitute of daily food, And one of you say unto them, Depart in peace, be ye warmed and filled; notwithstanding, ye give them not those things which are needful to the body, what does it profit? (James 2:15, 16).

The implication is obvious. It behooves Christians to be merciful. We're all to be showing kindness, yet some have the gift of showing mercy, to minister to the whole body.

The gift of exhortation. The Greek word translated "exhortation" refers to the deed done by one who comes along to help. Exhortation is not standing in the pulpit browbeating people. It's not necessarily a public gift though it may be used as such (I Cor. 14:3). The gift of exhortation is the ability to get alongside someone and comfort him with love. Jesus said,

> I will pray the Father, and he shall give you another Comforter, that he may abide with you for ever (John 14:16).

The Comforter is the Holy Spirit. The word "Comforter" is *paracletos,* "one called alongside." The believer with the gift of exhortation, in the power of the true Paraclete, the Holy Spirit, is used by the Spirit to come alongside members of the body to minister comfort, consolation, encouragement, counsel, and exhortation. This is the gift that qualifies people to exercise a counseling ministry in the body. Again, although there are some who have this gift, all Christians are to put their arms around each other. "But exhort one another daily" (Heb. 3:13). We're to put our arms around each other every day and comfort and counsel and share.

The gift of giving. This third love gift has direct

147

reference to the material ministry: food, clothes, money, houses, whatever it is that you desire to give. This is a Spirit-given gift. It is related to the Holy Spirit's supervision of everything a Christian possesses. It doesn't relate at all to how much he has; some of the people with the gift of giving are the poorest around. The gift has nothing to do with how much you have in your pocketbook, but only with the sovereignty of the Spirit of God, who gives the gift of giving. This gift is to provide for others who cannot supply their own needs. If those who have the gift would release themselves and use it in the energy of the Spirit, Christians could take care of all material needs in the body. Of course, the Bible commands that no Christian should miss the joy of giving.

> Every man according as he purposeth in his heart, so let him give; not grudgingly, or of necessity: for God loveth a cheerful giver (II Cor. 9:7).

The gifts of administration. These gifts belong to those in places of spiritual authority. Pastors, teachers, or evangelists exercise this gift. Note, for example, I Thessalonians 5:12:

> We beseech you, brethren, to know them which labour among you, and are over you in the Lord, and admonish you.

Some Christians have the place of being over others, to care for them—not to lord it over them, or to hammer them down, or to brutally subject them, but to teach them and instruct them (I Pet. 5:1-4). Also, I Timothy 5:17:

> Let the elders that rule well be counted worthy of double honour, especially they who labour in the word and doctrine.

The same teaching is found in Hebrews 13:7, 17, and 24:

> Remember them which have the rule over you, who have spoken unto you the word of God: whose faith

148

follow, considering the end of their conversation [manner of life]. . . . Obey them that have the rule over you, and submit yourselves: for they watch for your souls, as they that must give account. . . . Salute [greet] all them that have the rule over you.

The pastor, or elder, who has been given oversight of the flock must exercise the gift of government or ruling. In New Testament terms, I am, in my church, an elder. I'm not a "reverend." I happen to be an elder called by God to teach the Word and, consequently, to have the responsibility of spiritual ruling.

Of course, this gift is not limited to pastors in local churches. It is also exercised by those in leadership in Christian ministries like mission societies, youth works, and evangelistic associations.

The gift of ministry, or helps. Both of these terms mean service; these are gifts of assistance. The early deacons had this gift (the word translated "deacon" means service). Christians with this gift are helpers, persons who labor behind the scenes. If a Christian doesn't have the gift of teaching, he is to serve the body in another capacity and will find the Spirit of God energizing him, producing love and a feeling of oneness. This gift, like all the others, is to be to some degree evident in all Christians. All Christians are called to serve. "By love serve one another" (Gal. 5:13). Yet some are especially grace-gifted for service to the body.

We have noted briefly eleven edifying gifts. Now here is the key to all of them: every gift was characteristic of Jesus Christ. He had everyone of them in its fullness. He was preacher; He was teacher; He was faithful; He was wisdom personified; He was knowledge in the flesh; He was the discerner of spirits. He showed mercy; He was the true paraclete; He was the giver; He gave more than anyone ever gave; He was ruler and leader; and He was servant and minister. If you make a composite of these eleven gifts, you have a picture of Jesus Christ.

The church, a new body formed by Christ, is to do just what Christ's fleshly body did—manifest His nature. Since all these gifts were part of His fleshly body, all are also a part of His spiritual body. These gifts are the reproduction of Christ's attributes. They are now in the new body of Christ. They are grace gifts, given to the church by the Holy Spirit, so that the church may be the continuing life of Christ.

The reason every Christian should share in all these ministries to some degree is that all are called to be like Jesus Christ. Everything that characterized Him should be true also, though imperfectly, of every believer. If the Christian's testimony is to be totally effective, the world will have to see in him the very reflection of Jesus Christ Himself. It is vitally important for every believer to know his spiritual gift, and to use it, so that the body's witness might be effective, and so that each member in a personal way might exercise all of Christ's attributes.

b. Temporary gifts. The temporary gifts were not designed for the edification of the body, but for confirming the testimony of the apostles and prophets, that in fact they were declaring the Word of God. *Four* such gifts are listed in Scripture: miracles, healing, tongues, and interpretation of tongues. They have no continuing role in the body. They existed for the apostolic era and were designed for unbelievers—not believers—so that unbelievers might be convinced that the Word of God was being spoken by the apostles and prophets of the early church.

If many people spoke and there were no standard to judge them, people would not know what to believe. So, along with the truth speakers, along with the true apostles and prophets, there were certain miraculous gifts given so that people might be convinced that what they heard was true.

This principle is stated several places in Scripture. Mark 16:17 says,

> And these signs shall follow them that believe; In my name shall they cast out devils; they shall speak with new tongues.

Some miracles attended the initial preaching of the apostles. The people who responded to the apostles in that initial phase of the church saw the miracles happen. Further, Mark 16:19-20:

> So then after the Lord had spoken unto them [the apostles], he was received up into heaven, and sat on the right hand of God. And they went forth, and preached everywhere, the Lord working with them, and confirming the word with signs following.

"Signs" *(semeion)* always means "miracles." Miracles accompanied the apostles for the purpose of confirming the Word. II Corinthians 12:12 says,

> Truly the signs of an apostle were wrought among you in all patience, in signs, and wonders, and mighty deeds.

Signs of an apostle, a specific designation for miracles. Hebrews 2:3 says,

> How shall we escape, if we neglect so great salvation; which at the first began to be spoken by the Lord, and was confirmed unto us by them that heard him.

The message of salvation initially was spoken by Christ Himself, and confirmed by the apostles. "God also bearing them witness" (Heb. 2:4); "Them" refers to the apostles. "Both with signs and wonders, and with divers miracles, and gifts of the Holy Spirit" (v. 4). Apostles did miracles to confirm the Word. The miracles actually belonged to apostles; certain gifts of the Spirit were for the apostles. So the miraculous gifts mentioned in I Corinthians 12:28 are the signs and wonders and mighty deeds that belonged to the apostles, for the purpose of confirming the Word, establishing its veracity in the minds of persons who had no other standard. There was no written Word of God. There was not yet the accumulated standard of the New Testament. Signs were the confirmation of the Word; they were to ratify or establish the truth.

In the early church, the signs were a necessary adjunct to the preaching and teaching of the apostles and the early prophets. These gifts were evidently often passed on by the laying on of hands. In fact, there is no indication in the New Testament that anyone had these gifts other than by the laying on of hands of the apostles. B. B. Warfield says,

> These miraculous gifts were part of the credentials of the Apostles, as the authoritative agents of God in founding the church. Their function thus confines them to distinctly the Apostolic church and they necessarily passed away with it.

Certain passages specifically associate these miraculous gifts of the Spirit with the work of apostles. Note these examples:

> "Long time therefore abode they speaking boldly in the Lord, which gave testimony unto the word of his grace [These were New Testament prophets speaking the Word of the Lord.], and granted signs and wonders to be done by their hands" (Acts 14:3).

The Lord attested the veracity of their word by granting them signs and wonders. These words describe the activity of Paul and Barnabas when they went to Iconium during Paul's first missionary journey. God verified His truth by enabling them to do miracles. Note also Romans 15:15-19a:

> Nevertheless, brethren, I have written the more boldly unto you in some sort, as putting you in mind, because of the grace that is given to me of God, That I should be the minister of Jesus Christ to the Gentiles, ministering the gospel of God, that the offering up of the Gentiles might be acceptable, being sanctified by the Holy Ghost. I have therefore whereof I may glory through Jesus Christ in those things which pertain to God. For I will not dare to speak of any of those things which Christ hath not wrought by me, to make the Gentiles obedient, by word and deed, through mighty signs and wonders, by the power of the Spirit of God.

Paul said he spoke only what Christ told him to speak; his ministry was verified by signs and wonders. These miracles had nothing to do with believers; they were to confirm the Word to unbelievers.

From these passages we learn that the purpose and function of the special miraculous gifts of the Spirit was to authenticate the apostles as true messengers from the true God, and thus confirm the Gospel of salvation in the minds of unbelievers. The church today no longer needs this kind of confirmation. Believers do not need miracles as a standard by which to verify a person's teaching. They don't need someone to stand up and preach, then do a miracle so they will know he's telling the truth. Christians today have another standard—the Word of God. When someone preaches, we measure him by the Word of God. If he does not stand that test, we know that he is not a true teacher, but a false teacher even if miracles are present. The Bible itself is our confirmation. Abraham told the rich man in Hades, "If they hear not Moses and the prophets, neither will they be persuaded, though one rose from the dead" (Luke 16:31). If the Word of God isn't sufficient, miracles won't change a person's mind. Where the written Word of God is available, confirming miracles are irrelevant.

No miraculous confirming gift is mentioned in Ephesians 4, where the gifted men are mentioned. Paul's first letter to the Corinthians is the only one that mentions miraculous temporary gifts. In no other letter does he say that pastors, evangelists, or teachers should have any of these gifts. If the confirming gifts of the Word were still needed, they would be given to the men who preach the Word. What would be the point of giving confirming gifts to people who aren't preachers? If, in fact, these gifts still exist, they should belong to the great preachers and teachers in the world, because these are the men who are speaking, and they are the men whose message has to be confirmed. If these gifts were still given, would they be given to people who are out of the mainstream of the body, majoring in emotional experiences?

So, to conclude this introduction to the subject, we have seen that the *temporary sign gifts* were for the apostolic era. When the apostles and prophets passed away, so did the need for confirmation, because the Bible then became the standard. These gifts were never designed to belong to the edification of the body.

The gift of miracles. To say that miracles have ceased would be untrue. When I say that the gift of miracles has ceased, I do not mean that God doesn't do miracles. God is a God of miracles; He does great miracles today. The greatest kind of miracle God ever does is to take a degenerate, debased, sin-sick soul headed for hell, turn it around, and recreate it so that it becomes a citizen of heaven. But this is not to say that the gift of miracles still exists. It is no longer a gift through a person. God still does miracles by His own sovereign design and as a result of prayer; but this is not the same as the apostolic gift of miracles.

Jesus did many different kinds of miracles, including raising the dead. They were proofs of His deity. They were to verify His Messiahship; they were to substantiate His claim that He was the Son of God. But in His ministry miracles had a very limited effect. Not only did people refuse to believe Him, they also finally concluded that He did His miracles by Beelzebub, Satan.

Miracles also had a limited effect with the apostles and the prophets. The restoration of the lame person at Lystra by Paul seemed at first to have a great effect on the people, but soon after they stoned Paul and left him for dead. Paul's casting out of the evil spirit at Philippi was the direct cause of serious trouble. After this event, for a period of two years, there is no mention of Paul working any miracles.

There is no record of miracles happening at Antioch, at Corinth, at Thessalonica, at Derbe, at Berea. Paul put no emphasis on them; instead, he constantly stressed the need for faith. In his lists of requirements for bishops, elders, and deacons, he does not mention the gift of miracles. Throughout the epistles there is no emphasis on miracles.

Miracles had no continuing place in the ministry of the church. I am not depreciating miracles. They may still occur as God wills, but not through the *gift* of miracles, which was apostolic. They not only had a limited effect, they had a limited purpose. They were for the infancy stage of the church to verify the Gospel. They were the signs and wonders and mighty deeds just for the beginning. This principle is evident in Scripture. There were four periods of miracles in the Bible: first, in Moses' day; second, the time of Elijah and Elisha; third, the life of Christ; fourth, right after the life of Christ, in the early church after Pentecost. These periods of miracles show that their place is to attest to God's truth at a specific time, and they are always limited by time. Of course, God worked miracles at other times also, but where they were performed by individuals it was generally in these four periods. God still does miracles today, but not to authenticate His Word. It seems best to say that He does them apart from any gift of any man, in response to faith and prayer, and according to His own sovereign design.

The gift of healing. The gift of healing was the ability to heal whenever the opportunity presented itself. A man actually had the gift to heal people; it wasn't his own power. Peter said to the lame man, "In the name of Jesus Christ of Nazareth rise up and walk" (Acts 3:6). It was not their own power, but they were able to call on the power of Christ at any time to heal. Healing purposed to verify the Word; it was a confirming gift for unbelievers. God in His grace still heals. We have prayed for people, and God has healed them of diseases when they were past the point of recovery medically speaking. However, the gift of healing as such ceased with the apostolic era. Today God heals in His sovereign will in response to the prayer of faith. I believe there is a gift that brings about healing—the gift of faith. It is the same as the gift of prayer. This gift results in healing. God often heals in answer to prayer.

And again, if the gift of healing existed today, it would belong to people who are teachers of the Word. But instead, some of the people who claim the gift of healing often are inadequate preachers of the Bible. They often are confused in their theology. They frequently are self-styled "salesmen" operating on a performance basis.

Although we can't deny claims to gifts of healing, it is possible that a person who thinks he has healing really has the gift of faith. God responds to their prayer. My purpose is not to explain all cases of supposed healing; all I want to do is indicate the biblical teaching. The true gift of healing was to confirm the teaching and preaching of apostles and prophets. But today it is claimed by some people who are ignorant of the Word of God.

The apostolic gift of healing ceased, and the New Testament writers knew it. In the later years of the apostles' ministry, this gift began to disappear. The people who were sick stayed sick. God did not heal Paul. Timothy was sick; he probably had an ulcer. Did Paul tell him to find the one who has the gift of healing? No! He told him to take a little wine. There was the case of Trophimus, who was sick at Miletus (II Tim. 4:20). Paul left him there sick. If Paul had the gift of healing (and he had healed previously), would he not have exercised it on behalf of Trophimus?

The epistle of James was written long before I Corinthians. James tells what to do when somebody gets sick. He does not say, "Go to the healer; find the person who has the gift of healing." Rather, James says, "Is any among you afflicted? let him pray" (5:13). It says *pray,* not call on the man who has the gift of healing.

> Let him call for the elders of the church; and let them pray over him, anointing him with oil in the name of the Lord: and the prayer of faith shall save the sick (James 5:14, 15).

This is thought by many to refer to medicine. James, before I Corinthians was ever written, knew by inspiration of the Holy Spirit that in years to come the apostolic gift of healing would be nonexistent. The wisest counsel he could give the church was to seek by faith the healing that God offers. Having the elders pray and anoint with oil is the biblical approach to healing.

We must remember that the gift of healing was a sign to unbelievers. There seems to be no indication in the New Testament church that the gift of healing was ever experienced in behalf of the established Christians—it was always a sign to unbelievers.

The only word in the epistles related to healing in the church is James 5:14-16, and some scholars think this word is especially pertinent to Jewish Christians who might still claim the healing covenant promised in Exodus 15:26. Paul made no such blanket statement to the Gentile church—"the prayer of faith *shall* save the sick" (James 5:15, italics added). In the other epistles it is obvious that God allows certain sickness for His refining or chastening purposes. God does heal today, but not by a gift or covenant. It is by His sovereign will in each case. That does not make healing today any less miraculous!

The gift of tongues and the interpretation of tongues. We will cover the third and fourth gifts together (I Cor. 12:10). We will consider several questions related to these gifts. At the outset I want to say that I have great love in my heart for every believer in the body of Christ, whether he speaks in tongues or not. I say this honestly and not to be patronizing. I have some dear friends whom I love greatly, and they know Jesus Christ in a vital and real way. They have successful ministries that God is blessing, but they err when it comes to tongues. Remember, however, that there are many errors more serious than this. Gossip, for instance, is linked with murder and other things in the New Testament. Unfortunately, some Christians think that if a person speaks in tongues he is a gross heretic. I do not chastize people who do, but I feel there is a doctrinal position that I must hold from the Word of God. All I want to do is declare what this position is. I want to be faithful to God's Word.

What was the gift of tongues? What was its use? It was a Holy Spirit-given ability to speak a foreign language, to declare the wonderful works of God, a miracle of verification.

> And when the day of Pentecost was fully come, they were all with one accord in one place. And suddenly there came a sound from heaven as of a rushing mighty wind, and it filled all the house where they were sitting. And there appeared unto them cloven tongues like as of fire, and it sat upon each of them. And they were all filled with the Holy Ghost, and began to speak with other tongues [the Greek word is *glossa*—languages], as the Spirit gave them utterances (Acts 2:1-4).

It was the feast of Pentecost. Devout Jews came to Jerusalem from all over the Roman world. It was seemingly the perfect time to declare the wonderful works of God—at the birth of the church. What better time could there be, with all those foreigners there? You could tell them the truth, and they could take it back to their own countries. So the Christians spoke in all the various languages represented.

Now when this was noised abroad, the multitude

came together, and were confounded, because every man heard them speak in his own language (Acts 2:6).

God provided a miracle by which the believers could communicate to persons in their own languages. The miraculous element attested to the truthfulness of the message of Christ's death and resurrection. The people were singularly impressed.

We do hear them speak in our tongues the wonderful works of God. And they were all amazed and were perplexed, saying one to another, What meaneth this? (Acts 2:11, 12).

Tongues-speaking was a declaration of the wonderful works of God.

Speaking this way did not substitute for preaching, because right after the tongues experience came Peter's sermon. Tongues were not necessary to preach the Gospel, and they were not to convict of sin. They were merely to attest that God was going to speak.

Elsewhere in Acts, speaking in tongues followed the same pattern. It occurred next in Samaria. The background is that the Jews hated the Samaritans, who were a mixed race. However, after the Samaritans received the Gospel, the apostles from Jerusalem went to Samaria. When the apostles arrived, they

prayed for them, that they might receive the Holy Ghost: (For as yet he was fallen upon none of them: only they were baptized in the name of the Lord Jesus.) Then laid they their hands on them, and they received the Holy Ghost (Acts 8:15-17).

At that point, I assume, the people spoke in tongues because it would have been very easy for the Jewish believers to say, "Well, you Samaritans, we are not getting together with you on any common ground." If the miracle of tongues occurred for the Jews of Pentecost, the same miracle would occur in Samaria. Otherwise, the Jews would not accept the Samaritans into fellowship. Tongues had to happen in Samaria for the benefit of the Jews, that they might know that the church was to be one.

After Samaria, the Gospel reached the Gentile world in the person of Cornelius. "While Peter yet spake these words, the Holy Ghost fell on all them which heard the word. And they of the circumcision which believed were astonished" (Acts 10:44, 45). The Jews were astonished "because that on the Gentiles also was poured out the gift of the Holy Ghost. For they heard them speak with tongues" (Acts 10:45, 46). The Gentiles had the same tongues experience that the Jews had had at Pentecost. It was important for the Gentiles to have it so that the Jews might know that Christ was starting a new body in which everyone was equal. Whether Jews, Samaritans, or Gentiles, they were one in Christ, so the same miracle of tongues happened when the Holy Spirit came on each group.

Acts 19 tells of a handful of people who had been saved under the old economy. They had repented, were baptized by John the Baptist, but did not know about Jesus.

> He [Paul] said unto them, Have ye received the Holy Ghost since ye believed? And they said unto him, We have not so much as heard whether there be any Holy Ghost. And he said unto them, Unto what then were ye baptized? And they said, Unto John's baptism. Then said Paul, John verily baptized with the baptism of repentance, saying unto the people, that they should believe on him who should come after him, that is, on Christ Jesus. When they heard this, they were baptized in the name of the Lord Jesus. And when Paul had laid his hands upon them, the Holy Ghost came on them; and they spake with tongues (Acts 19:2-6).

Why did these men speak with tongues, too? Because they needed the same miracle that occurred with the Jews, so that all of them would be one. There would be no inequality in the body. The mir-

160

acle of tongues occurred those four times in Acts, to bring everyone into the one fold.

When the miracles of tongues occurred, it was always a known language. It was never gibberish. It was a foreign language known to some present, though the speaker did not know it. The word used in Acts 2 means "language." Acts 10:46 says the Gentiles spoke with tongues and glorified God. The witnesses knew the Gentiles were glorifying God because it was a language they understood. Reporting this experience, Peter says, "Forasmuch then as God gave them the like gift as he did unto us" (Acts 11:17). Since the gift was known languages in Acts 2, when the Jews received it, it was known languages when the Gentiles received it. The same would be true for the disciples of John (Acts 19:6).

Paul speaks of various "kinds of tongues" (I Cor. 12:10). The word "kinds" is from the word *genos* from which we get our word "genus." *Genos* means a nation, a race, or a kind. "Kinds of tongues" therefore means specific national languages, races and languages. If the miracle of tongues is gibberish—not known languages—Paul's statement would be pointless. How can you have "kinds of gibberish"? Gibberish is gibberish, there are no kinds of it.

The companion gift is "the interpretation of tongues." The Greek word literally means "translation." But how can you translate gibberish? If someone had the gift of speaking known languages, someone else had the gift of translating them. In the King James Version of I Corinthians 14, where the word "unknown" precedes "tongues," it is always in italics. This means "unknown" was supplied by the translators—it is not in the original Greek text.

Also in I Corinthians 14, Paul says any use of tongues must be according to grammatical structure.

And even things without life giving sound, whether pipe or harp, except they give a distinction in the sounds, how shall it be known what is piped or harped? (I Cor. 14:7).

Some Corinthian believers were speaking gibberish; they were exercising a fleshly counterfeit of the real gift. Paul used music to prove that speaking in tongues means using a language with grammatical structure.

> Therefore if I know not the meaning of the voice, I shall be unto him that speaketh a barbarian, and he that speaketh shall be a barbarian unto me (I Cor. 14:11).

That means speaking gibberish.

Apparently, the miracle of tongues was a sign to Jews only. In I Corinthians 14:21 Paul quotes Isaiah 28:11, where the prophet predicted the gift of tongues as a God-given sign to the Jewish nation. He says,

> In the law it is written, With men of other tongues and other lips will I speak unto this people; and yet for all that will they not hear me, saith the Lord.

The expression "this people" can refer only to Israel. The gift may have been prominent in Corinth because it was a thriving, commercial center with a large Jewish element (Acts 18:1-17), but there was no point for the gift in the assembly of the Gentile church. Visiting Gentiles would think they were mad (I Cor. 14:23). In the case of tongues in Acts it was always for the benefit of the Jews that this occurred (cf. Acts 10:44-47).

God is not now giving signs to Israel in connection with the preaching of the Gospel, as in the first years of the church; this is one reason why I believe the sign of tongues has ceased.

It is wrong for Christians today to take the church at Corinth as their pattern for tongues. The Corinthians had perverted the true gift. The problems in Corinth were many: division, carnality, wrong concepts of the Gospel ministry, sexual perversion, lawsuits between Christians, moral misconduct of believers' bodies, abused marriage relationships, violation of Christian liberty, insubordination of women, evils at the Lord's Supper, ignorance of spiritual gifts, denial of the resurrection of the body. Believers ought not to take the Corinthians as their example for tongues.

The problem was not that the Corinthians lacked spiritual gifts. Paul says in I Corinthians 1:7 "Ye come behind in no gift." Rather, they abused the gifts. They had a unique problem because in that part of the world ecstatic speech prevailed among the frenzied priests and priestesses of pagan Greek religions. The Corinthian believers had been saved out of that, but evidently they took some of this pagan, ecstatic speech into their Christian experience. It counterfeited the true miracle of tongues. Paul wrote I Corinthians 12—14 in an effort to correct the Corinthian abuses of tongues.

Those abuses included subordinating tongues to preaching, and speaking in tongues without an interpreter. Paul says,

> Tongues are for a sign, not to them that believe, but to them that believe not: but prophesying serveth not for them that believe not, but for them which believe. If therefore the whole church be come together into one place, and all speak with tongues, and there come in those that are unlearned, or unbelievers, will they not say that ye are mad? But if all prophesy, and there come in one that believeth not, or one unlearned, he is convicted of all, he is judged of all (I Cor. 14:22-24).

The priority of preaching over tongues in the church is clearly seen here. Paul goes on to rebuke the believers at Corinth for confusion in their meetings. "If any man speak in an unknown tongue, let it be by two, or at the most by three ... and let one interpret" (14:27). Women were not to speak (14:34).

The big question, of course, is whether the apostolic miracle of tongues exists today. The statements

163

of I Corinthians 13:8-12 need to be studied carefully in this connection.

> Charity never faileth: but whether there be prophecies, they shall fail; whether there be tongues, they shall cease; whether there be knowledge, it shall vanish away. For we know in part, and we prophesy in part. But when that which is perfect is come, then that which is in part shall be done away (vv. 8-10).

Verse 8 indicates that prophecy and knowledge will be "rendered inoperative" (katargeo) and tongues will "cease" (pauo). Pauo is in the middle voice, which is reflexive—tongues will cease "by themselves." The verb is intransitive and doesn't take an object; this means the end of tongues is not some great event caused by something else—tongues will fade out by themselves. Katargeo is a transitive verb; something will halt prophecy and knowledge, will cause them to cease. That something is the "perfect" thing—the return of the Lord.

To illustrate this distinction in a literary way, Paul omits tongues from verses I Corinthians 13:9-12 and speaks only of prophecy and knowledge. They will remain unto Christ's second coming; tongues will not be around then, but will have already ceased.

The evidence of history, according to such scholars as Warfield, Hoekema, Cotten, and Gromacki, is that indeed the temporary sign gift of tongues has ceased.

Why, then, are so many people experiencing the so-called gift of tongues today? There are several reasons. Number one is a departure from systematic Bible interpretation. Many people just don't know any better doctrinally. Someone convinces them that "tongues" is the thing to seek. Second, many people are starved for the supernatural. Tongues gives them a kind of supernatural experience, something above their usual Christian experience. This leads to the third reason. People want a feeling of some kind; they want an emotional experience. The fourth reason people seek this is that they consider it a quick way to spirituality. Just speak in tongues and you are spiritual. They rest in their tongues experience; they go no further.

The modern tongues movement appears to me to have no basis in biblical doctrine. Subjective experience is its major defense: "It happened to me, therefore it must be real." That is not a valid test. The flesh and Satan can produce counterfeit experiences.

The modern movement confuses the doctrine of the baptism of the Holy Spirit. A true movement cannot be based on a false doctrine. Tongues people equate speaking in tongues with the baptism of the Holy Spirit, but I Corinthians 12:13 says, "For by one Spirit are we all baptized into one body." That happens at salvation; it is not a continuous thing. Biblically speaking, you can't say to a believer, "You don't have the Holy Spirit until you speak in tongues." Romans 8:9 says, "If any man have not the Spirit of Christ, he is none of his." I Corinthians 3:16 says, "Know ye not that ye are the temple of God, and that the Spirit of God dwelleth in you?" Every believer has the Spirit.

The new tongues movement also subordinates Christ to the Holy Spirit. It violates the Spirit's ministry, which is to exalt Christ. The tongues movement reverses this. By making Christians feel they are "second class" Christians until they speak in tongues, they subordinate Christ to the Holy Spirit. This creates two levels of Christians, the spiritual ones and the ones who haven't arrived. But in Christ there is no difference; Christians are one in the Spirit.

All gifts were to be exercised in love. Often, when "tongues" appear in a local church, instead of creating an atmosphere of love, the "gift" creates an atmosphere of friction and division that divides the church. Any legitimate gift of the Spirit, operated in the energy of the Spirit, brings unity.

Tongues advocates imply that the church had no power for 1800 years because the Holy Spirit's baptism wasn't experienced. However, Peter said all believers have "all things that pertain unto life and godliness" (II Pet. 1:3). Believers do not lack anything by not having any of the temporary sign gifts. God made provision for the confirmation of His Word in the nurturing of the infant church. Today, instead of seeking those things, believers ought to thank God that we don't need them anymore. We have the resources according to the standard of the Word of God; God authenticates His message today by His Word. If God chooses to give the miraculous ability of tongues today for a special purpose, it must square with all the biblical patterns, for "Jesus Christ [is] the same yesterday, and to day, and for ever" (Heb. 13:8). Members of the body are not told in Scripture to seek miraculous, temporary "sign" gifts, but rather to minister the edifying permanent grace gifts to one another that the body may grow to full stature.

Chapter Nine

THE FELLOWSHIP OF THE BODY

Because the church is one body, all its members are members of one another. It is like a human body with connected tissues, muscles, bones, ligaments, and organs. No member of the body of Christ exists detached from the rest of the body, no more than your lungs can lie on the floor in the next room and keep you breathing. No one member can escape his responsibility toward all the other members. The health of the body, its witness, and its testimony are dependent on the faithful ministering of all the members to one another.

The fact that we are believers in Christ means we are one in position. We have all been placed into the body of Christ by the Holy Spirit. Positional unity is manifest by the fact that the one same Spirit who placed believers into the body dwells within all believers (I Cor. 12:13). That is positional unity.

On the other side, we want to discuss practical unity. Though Christians are one in position, unfortunately they are not one in practice—in the nitty-gritty of living and loving together. Positional oneness

UNITY OF THE BODY

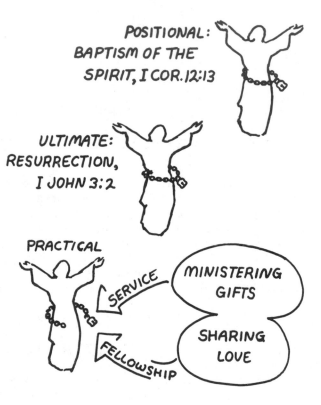

POSITIONAL:
BAPTISM OF THE
SPIRIT, I COR. 12:13

ULTIMATE:
RESURRECTION,
I JOHN 3:2

PRACTICAL

SERVICE

MINISTERING GIFTS

SHARING LOVE

FELLOWSHIP

There are three kinds of unity: positional unity, secured by the baptism of the Spirit; ultimate unity, secured by the Resurrection; and practical unity, which is presently unsecured but can be secured by the ministering of spiritual gifts and the sharing of love in fellowship.

does not guarantee oneness in practice. Jesus prayed in John 17:21, "that they all may be one." He was not just praying for positional oneness—that is accomplished by salvation. He was praying for Christians to live in oneness.

This practical, experiential unity of the body is manifest by two things: service and fellowship. By service we mean ministering our spiritual gifts to each other. Fellowship is sharing our love with each other. We have already considered service: the operation of spiritual gifts (Chapter Eight). Now we turn to fellowship.

The New Testament word for fellowship is *koinonia*. It means communion or fellowship—intimate communication. God designed men for fellowship. In Genesis 2:18, God says, "It is not good that the man should be alone." Man was not made to be isolated; being alone is not the will of God. People were made for fellowship. And the church, the body of Christ, is the epitome of fellowship—a body for fellowship! The church is a fellowship. The church was never intended to be only a building—a place where lonely people walk in, listen, and walk out still alone—but a place of fellowship.

Bruce Larson says,

> The neighborhood bar is possibly the best counterfeit there is to the fellowship Christ wants to give His Church. It's an imitation dispensing liquor instead of grace, escape rather than reality. But it is a permissive, accepting, and inclusive fellowship. It is unshockable, it is democratic. You can tell people secrets and they usually don't tell others, or want to. The bar flourishes not because most people are alcoholics, but because God has put into the human heart the desire to know and be known, to love, and be loved, and so many seek a counterfeit at the price of a few beers.[1]

This need for fellowship is the genius of the church.

[1] Bruce Larson, *Dare to Live Now!* (Grand Rapids: Zondervan, 1965), page 110.

But it is not met simply by the Sunday services—either by the small, closed group of persons who know nothing of a stranger, or the large mass aggregations of unrelated, disconnected people. Consequently, there exists in the church today a desperate need for personal, intimate fellowship. And this fellowship, like the ministering of the gifts, is intrinsic to the manifestation of our practical unity. Fellowship is essential to the life of the body. It is body life!

The New Testament teaches four things about fellowship: (1) its basis, what fellowship is founded upon; (2) its nature, what it's like; (3) its danger, what interrupts it; and (4) its responsibilities, what is necessary to maintain it.

1. *The basis of fellowship.* There is much phony fellowship today, people getting together on all kinds of pretenses. That is not true Christian fellowship. The basis of body fellowship is not the need of the community, or some common social or religious goal. The basis is indicated by the word *koinonia,* just "sharing a partnership, commonness, fellowship, communion." Do believers have a common ground? Are they partners in something? Do they have something they may share?

The ground of Christian fellowship is presented in I John 1:3,

That which we have seen and heard declare we unto you, that ye also may have fellowship with us: and truly our fellowship is with the Father, and with His Son Jesus Christ.

John relates the Gospel to that which he has personally experienced (v. 1). He gives his firsthand relationship with Jesus Christ. He proclaims the Gospel because the Gospel is the basis of fellowship. John is saying, "I want you to know the same God and the same Christ that I know, in order that we may have common ground for fellowship."

170

The proclamation of the Gospel is not an end in itself. What is the end? Fellowship! The preaching of the Gospel is supposed to create a fellowship (cf. Phil. 1:5). Not an organization, but a fellowship; not an organizational chart on a printed sheet, but a fellowship.

The beautiful, meaningful fellowship created by Christ and His disciples in the days when He was on earth was not to be limited just to them, but was to extend to all of us who came after and believed in Christ. We are to be introduced into that very same fellowship. In a sense, we are in the fellowship of the apostles—we are in their fellowship (note this in Ephesians 3 and Hebrews 2). But our fellowship is primarily with the Father and with His Son. We are all wrapped up in a total fellowship, involving the Father, the Son, the Spirit, and every other believer in history (Phil. 2:1; II Cor. 13:14; Eph. 4:4-6). Salvation made it happen.

There is no fellowship with God prior to salvation, or with Christ or His Spirit. There is no fellowship with believers until you become a believer. At that instant you enter fellowship with God and every other believer, and it is eternal.

It was God's design to bring us into fellowship. The Apostle Paul says,

God is faithful, by whom ye were called unto the fellowship of his Son Jesus Christ our Lord (I Cor. 1:9).

God is not some distant, cosmic deity. Through His sovereign grace He brought us into His fellowship, by faith in Jesus Christ. Paul speaks of "the common faith" (Titus 1:4). Every believer is part of a common faith, a single body of truth. Each came to God the same way—by faith.

Fellowship in this context becomes a specifically Christian word, referring to that common participation in the grace of God, the salvation of Christ, and

171

the blessing of the indwelling Spirit. The apostolic objective in all preaching was to create a human fellowship, rising spontaneously out of the divine fellowship. The divine fellowship existed, and because the divine fellowship reached down to man, a human fellowship came into being. Fellowship is not just one aspect of the body, but a goal of the whole Gospel.

In the purest sense, no Christian is at any time out of fellowship with God. You can't sever that relationship. Suppose, for example, that two people enter into marriage, a partnership. They may not be speaking to each other, yet the partnership continues. Or, there may be partners in business; they may not like each other, but they remain partners. This is an inadequate way of saying that the believer and God are in an eternal partnership. You may not really be acting like a partner with God; you may be violating some of the partnership standards. But the partnership maintains itself. Salvation ushers us into permanent fellowship with God. In Philippians 1:5 Paul refers to the "fellowship in the gospel" which continued "from the first day [salvation]" until the present.

Now we often say, when everything is going great and happy and kind of tuned into the Lord, "I'm in fellowship." But when you are not excited about the Lord, and there is sin in your life and indifference about your Christian experience, you say, "I'm out of fellowship." Strictly speaking, that is not true. You are always in fellowship; you are a partner with God.

But what happens when the believer sins? I John 1:4 says, "These things write we unto you, that your joy may be full." That is the issue—the difference in the partnership when there is full joy and when there is not full joy. If you want to evaluate your Christian life rightly, say it this way, "I'm experiencing full joy in my fellowship with the Father." Or, "I'm not experiencing the joy of my fellowship with God." In other words, the issue is not whether you are in or out of fellowship; it is whether or not you are experiencing full joy in that fellowship. The joy of our fellowship with God is affected by sin. If you are out of fellowship, in the theological sense, you are not saved. You have no partnership with God.

The basis of fellowship is stated this way in I John 1:9: "If we confess our sins, he is faithful and just to forgive us our sins, and to cleanse us from all unrighteousness." That kind of confession thus becomes the pattern of life. Believers do not need to keep on asking to be forgiven, but by the very nature of their salvation they open their hearts and admit to God what they are—sinful. The unbeliever confesses initially to be saved. A Christian constantly acknowledges his sin. Once he is in fellowship with God, it is the pattern of his life to acknowledge sin.

2. *The nature of fellowship.* The nature of fellowship may be seen from several New Testament examples.

> And the multitude of them that believed were of one heart and of one soul: neither said any of them that aught [any] of the things which he possessed was his own; but they had all things common. . . . Neither was there any among them that lacked: for as many as were possessors of lands or houses sold them, and brought the prices of the things that were sold, And laid them down at the apostles' feet: and distribution was made unto every man according as he had need (Acts 4:32, 34, 35).

They shared everything. They had everything in common—that was true fellowship.

This fellowship has a marked effect on the world. Many persons were brought to Christ.

> With great power gave the apostles witness of the resurrection of the Lord Jesus: and great grace was upon them all (Acts 4:33).

> And all that believed were together, and had all things common; And sold their possessions and goods, and parted them to all men, as every man had need.

173

And they, continuing daily with one accord in the temple, and breaking bread from house to house, did eat their meat with gladness and singleness of heart, Praising God, and having favour with all the people. And the Lord added to the church daily such as should be saved (Acts 2:44-47).

This was the oneness that Christ had prayed for. Because the world could see this unity and love, people were the more readily convinced of the identity of Jesus Christ.

Paul describes a later example of fellowship among churches. "For it hath pleased them of Macedonia and Achaia to make a certain contribution for the poor saints which are at Jerusalem." The wealthier church in Europe collected money to send to poorer Christians. In Christian fellowship there is a spirit of bearing one another's burdens, sharing needs, and teaching (Rom. 1:11, 12; Gal. 6:2, 6). Those early Christians enjoyed a fellowship of money, food, homes, prayer, love, spiritual blessing, and teaching.

Paul himself needed this kind of fellowship. He didn't just zip through the world all by himself. "Nevertheless God, that comforteth those that are cast down, comforted us by the coming of Titus" (II Cor. 7:6). Paul's heart was blessed by fellowship. He told Timothy, "Do thy diligence to come shortly unto me; . . . Do thy diligence to come before winter" (II Tim. 4:9, 21). He cherished fellowship, he longed for it. Theirs was a love fellowship, and Paul hungered for it.

What is Christian fellowship today? Is it going to "fellowship hall" in the church basement, or a picnic or a Sunday school class party? Is it a meeting? Fellowship can happen anywhere, under any circumstance. All it means is that Christians begin to get involved with each other, sharing love around the Word of God, in the energy of the Holy Spirit. Sometimes after I have been with Christians I write it off as a wasted evening. Other times, I have experienced true fellowship in the Word and the things of God, so that I have come away warmed in spirit.

In true fellowship Christians don't judge one another, they don't bite and devour each other, they don't provoke, envy, lie to one another, speak evil, grumble about one another. Those are the New Testament principles. But what are the positives? Since true fellowship builds up, it means Christians receive one another, they are kind to one another, tenderhearted to one another, forbear and forgive one another, serve one another, practice hospitality ungrudgingly to one another, admonish, instruct, submit to one another, comfort one another. That is the true fellowship of the body.

3. *The danger to fellowship.* Fellowship with God is never broken because it is an eternal partnership (John 10:28, 29). But since God is holy, sin—while not eliminating the partnership—destroys the joy of the fellowship. Thus I John 1:4 says, "These things write we unto you, that your joy may be full." Sin is deadly to the joy of fellowship. When a believer is in sin, the one thing he doesn't want to do is get near the things of God, because he comes under conviction. When sin comes in, he loses the joy of communion with God. Usually his prayer life goes, his Bible reading goes, he drifts away from other Christians and their relationship—all because he doesn't want to be confronted with God.

If a Christian sins willfully and continually, he has purposely broken trust with God. He has willfully spurned His love, and although that does not break the partnership, it destroys the joy of fellowship. If I sin, that doesn't change God's love for me; it doesn't even mean I don't love Him. It does mean I'm not walking in the joy of pure fellowship. The principle is obvious: if God is light and sin is darkness, then when the believer sins, he loses the joy of his fellowship.

175

The symbol of body fellowship is the Communion service. When Christians meet around the Lord's table and partake of the cup and the bread, they are symbolizing His death which is the basis of fellowship. The word *koinonia* in Greek includes both fellowship and communion. Paul writes,

> The cup of blessing which we bless, is it not the communion of the blood of Christ? The bread which we break, is it not the communion of the body of Christ? ... Ye cannot drink the cup of the Lord, and the cup of devils; ye cannot be partakers of the Lord's table, and of the table of devils (I Cor. 10:16, 21).

How could Christians drink of the cup of the Lord, celebrate their fellowship with Him, and then go out and fellowship with demons? That makes a mockery of the Cross. Sin is communion with Satan and his fallen angels. It is blasphemous to do that while also going to the Lord's table to celebrate with Him of His body. So Paul warns,

> Let a man examine himself, and so let him eat of that bread, and drink of that cup. For he that eateth and drinketh unworthily, eateth and drinketh damnation to himself, not discerning the Lord's body (I Cor. 11:28, 29).

How does God judge a believer who does that?

> For this cause many are weak and sickly among you, and many sleep (11:30).

Some of them even died.

What am I saying? Just this: the Lord's table is the common symbol of Christian fellowship because it symbolizes the Cross which brought believers into the fellowship. When a believer was living in a pattern of sin, he was thereby forbidden to enter into this experience of Communion. Why? Because his sin had violated all that the Cross stood for, his participation would have been a mockery serious enough, in fact, to cause his own death. That is why Paul says, "Before you go to the Lord's table, you had better examine yourself carefully, to be sure that you are not at the same time celebrating or fellowshiping with demons." Sin was such a danger to fellowship that this kind of people was restricted from participating in Communion.

Sin breaks the joy of a Christian's fellowship with other believers as well as with the Lord. It shatters the unity of the body. Your sin affects me because it limits my fellowship, and it limits the use of your gifts in my behalf. A Christian can't say, "It doesn't bother me, I can do what I want, it won't affect anybody else." Sin in a believer's life causes a crippling of the body, at that point eliminating fellowship which is so needed. Pride, lust, materialism, failure to minister your gift, ceasing to pray, spiritual laziness, not yielding to the Holy Spirit—all these and every other sin destroy fellowship in the body.

The sins that believers daily open to God in confession and willingly acknowledge, however, do not become the pattern established in their lives and thus do not affect the fellowship as continuous, prolonged sin does. I find that if I sin and immediately acknowledge my sin to God and repent in godly sorrow, the joy of my fellowship is unbroken. But when sin persists, the joy of fellowship is destroyed. Repentance really is necessary for the joy of fellowship. The danger to fellowship, then, is sin without repentance. We see that the basis of fellowship is salvation, the nature of it is unity, and the danger to it is sin.

4. *The responsibilities of fellowship.* What is our obligation to other believers in terms of fellowship? How do we maintain it with other believers? We have already seen that it is necessary to bring sin before the Lord, acknowledge it, confess it, and repent of it. But apart from that we maintain fellowship by doing certain things for other believers. They are the "one anothers" of the New Testament.

Confess your faults one to another. James 5:16 says:

"Confess your faults one to another, and pray one for another." The word translated "fault" is the Greek word *hamartia,* the chief biblical word for sin. One way to maintain the fellowship of the body of Christ is to confess your sins to other Christians. Imagine what a depth of honesty, beauty, and understanding would be brought to Christian fellowship if believers could openly share their sins. They ought to be able to know that when they share a problem, their fellow Christian will say, "That's amazing; that's the same problem I have." Think how much more intelligently believers could pray for and minister to each other if they knew they had the same problem.

Too often, however, Christians put little glass bubbles around themselves and try to look like supersaints, as if they hadn't a single problem in the world. They are not willing to share openly, to expose their sins and problems to a fellow believer. They are not willing to sit down with another Christian and tell what their needs and problems are. They don't know what it is to have another believer put his arm around them and say, "You know, that's the same thing I'm going through. You pray for me and I'll pray for you."

The value of this is that when a believer is confronted with a temptation, he can think of all the people he shared his problem with who have the same problem. That gives him a solid basis for resistance to sin and Satan. Recently a brother in Christ confessed a sin to me and promised to do so each time he commits it. He told me just that promise has prevented it from happening again.

James knew what he was talking about when he said, "Confess your faults one to another." That is not only good psychological therapy, but spiritually it is a tremendous preventative to sin. Somewhere along the line Christians need to break through their isolation, crucify their egos, and begin to share and confess their faults one to another. There is no priesthood here except the priesthood of believers. This confession is *one* believer to *one* other—not publicly before either the whole church or the world.

Particularly if a believer has wronged a brother in Christ, he should go to him. Matthew 5:23, 24 says,

Therefore if thou bring thy gift to the altar, and there rememberest that thy brother hath aught [anything] against thee; Leave there thy gift before the altar, and go thy way; first be reconciled to thy brother, and then come and offer thy gift.

You don't pay homage to God until you have made everything right with other believers.

Confession of sin to each other maintains a pure fellowship and builds a common bond of people who know and love each other and understand each other's needs, anxieties, temptations and sins. That is each Christian's responsibility in the body. What strength Christians would find in that kind of community!

Forgive one another. Not only do Christians confess their sins one to another, but they forgive each other. Some Christians have a hard time doing that. You hear them say, "Well, if somebody ever did that to me, I'd never forgive them!" Such an attitude is unworthy of a Christian.

II Corinthians 2:6 says, "Sufficient to such a man is this punishment." This means that fellow Christians are not to hold sin over a brother's head the rest of his life. On the contrary,

ye ought rather to forgive him, and comfort him, lest perhaps such a one should be swallowed up with overmuch sorrow. Wherefore I beseech you that ye would confirm your love toward him (2:7, 8).

If a person is taken in sin, he is going to have enough problems with the consequences of sin without other Christians holding it over his head. They are to go to him and forgive him.

Paul adds, "Forbearing one another, and forgiving one another, if any man have a quarrel against any; even as Christ forgave you" (Col. 3:13). No one deserves to be forgiven by Christ. So it is not right to accept Christ's forgiveness and then refuse to extend forgiveness to a fellow Christian (cf. Eph. 4:32).

Forgiveness balances confession. When someone comes and confesses, you forgive. If someone confesses, "I just want you to know that for ten years I've hated you. I've been talking behind your back," the Christian reaction is forgiveness. When there is that kind of mutual concern in the body of Christ, great things will happen.

Bear one another's burdens. Galatians 6:2 says, "Bear ye one another's burdens, and so fulfil the law of Christ." A Christian can't bear someone's burden unless that fellow Christian shares them with him. Christians start by confessing their faults, forgiving each other, and then carrying each other's burdens. That means sympathetically loving one another.

Rebuke sin in one another. What should a Christian do when he sees a believer sinning? Don't say anything to him? Don't embarrass him? Ephesians 5:11 says, "And have no fellowship with the unfruitful works of darkness, but rather reprove them." If a Christian sees a brother who is sinning, he has the spiritual obligation to tell him so—in love. This is a serious thing. Paul says, even in reference to an elder, "Them that sin rebuke before all, that others also may fear" (I Tim. 5:20).

Imagine what would happen if I called Mr. So-and-so in front of others and said, "Now I want to tell you what you did. . . ." If our fellowship in the body were really working, this would tend to have an immediate purifying effect on us all. However, most Christians are afraid to exercise this responsibility. If they discover someone else's sin, they gasp and keep it to themselves, or they gossip about it.

Occasionally someone will come to me and say, "You know, pastor, I don't know if you've heard, but Mr. So-and-so is doing such-and-such." When that happens, I say, "Have you talked to him about it?"

If a Christian sees a brother in a sin, he is to rebuke him, remembering that the brother has the same obligation. The point of this is not only to restrict sin, but also to get Christians to open up and be themselves with each other. The church is a fellowship where every body-member ministers. We need to be ready to rebuke sin in each other. Paul said to Titus in regard to certain Christians in Crete: "Wherefore rebuke them sharply, that they may be sound in the faith" (Titus 1:13). If you find someone teaching false doctrine, tell him so.

> These things speak, and exhort, and rebuke with all authority. Let no man despise thee (Titus 2:15).

You do it, and don't let men despise you for it. The Christian who is Spirit-filled has the right to go to a sinning brother and openly rebuke him for his sins. That leads to pure fellowship; that purifies the ranks.

Restore the sinning brother.

> If a man be overtaken in a fault, ye which are spiritual, restore such an one in the spirit of meekness; considering thyself, less thou also be tempted (Gal. 6:1).

Once we have rebuked him, it is time to restore him. Pick him up and say, "Now let me show you from the Word of God what is going on. Let's have prayer together. Let's get back on the right track." That is restoration. This is caring for him. A Christian hasn't done his duty if all he has done is rebuke; he needs to restore, in love.

Take special care for the weaker brother. Believers are not to offend the weaker brother. They are not to abuse their liberty and thus cause offense (note particularly Romans 14:13, 19).

Love equally with no favoritism. Equal love is the theme of Paul's thought in Romans 12:10, 16; 13:8; 15:5, 7. It is the central thrust of Christian fellowship. The fellowship of the body is shattered when love has any preference. Love for all without favorites must be cultivated. This means esteeming all above yourself. John said, "Beloved, let us love one another" (I John 4:7).

Peter called for this when he wrote, "See that ye love one another with a pure heart fervently" (I Pet. 1:22). "Fervently" is a word from the medical vocabulary; it means "stretched." Christians are to stretch their love like a muscle extended to reach all. Peter further defined this kind of equal, stretched love as compassionate (3:8), hospitable to strangers (4:9), submissive (5:5), and physically demonstrative (5:14).

This kind of love should include caring service for each other (Gal. 5:13); patience and long-suffering (Eph. 4:2; Col. 3:13); and result in kindness, tender-heartedness, and forgiveness (Eph. 4:32; Col. 3:13).

Comfort and exhort one another. This is mentioned in several Scriptures. Paul, writing to the discouraged Thessalonian believers, encourages them to "comfort one another" (I Thess. 4:18; 5:11). Twice in Hebrews (3:13; 10:25) the injunction is given to "exhort one another." "Comfort" and "exhort" come from the same Greek word, *parakaleo*. It means "to come alongside to help." This is the ministry of personal counsel. It seems to be presented in light of the brevity of time. In Thessalonians, it is used in the context of the Rapture; in Hebrews, the context is coming judgment. It is an urgent word. Christians are to help each other with personal counsel in view of the coming of Jesus (cf. Rev. 22:12).

Discipline. The responsibility of discipline belongs not to the individual, but to the local assembly. The local church has the responsibility, when someone continues in sin, to put that person out of the church. Paul told the Corinthians "to deliver such an one unto Satan" (I Cor. 5:5). Paul told Timothy that he was delivering Hymenaeus and Alexander to Satan, that they might learn not to blaspheme (I Tim. 1:20).

We usually think the sinning believer needs to be in church, but the Bible says to put him out. Sin destroys the purity of the fellowship! A believer continuing in sin must be brought to the place of repentance before God so that he does not corrupt the fellowship. In Matthew 18 Jesus gives the pattern for such dismissal. The body cannot tolerate sin. In the early church, sinning brothers were put out in two ways: they were eliminated from the Lord's table, and they were put out of the fellowship of other believers. They were still regarded as Christians, but they were removed lest they taint the fellowship.

Three "one anothers" make a fitting conclusion for this chapter. The first one is to "edify one another" (Rom. 14:19; I Thess. 5:11). The tool for this is the Word of God. Paul commended the Ephesian elders "to God, and to the word of his grace, which is able to build you up" (Acts 20:32). Christians have a far-reaching responsibility to know the Word, not only for their own sakes but so that they may build up each other. Every Christian has a personal responsibility to know the Word of God so that he may use it in instructing other believers. Personal ignorance of Scripture brings corporate damage to the body.

The second is "to admonish one another" (Rom. 15:14; Col. 3:16). Apparently, this kind of encouraging counsel implies sin is present, which needs warning and discipline. It means encouraging a brother in sin to live righteously and godly. Admonishing is never harsh, unloving, or abusive. It is to be done gently (cf. II Thess. 3:14, 15).

The third "one another" is in James 5:16: "Pray one for another." This responsibility is at the heart of relationships in the body. It is something no Christian may avoid and still be a contributing member of the body. Such mutual prayer is based on the honest sharing of personal needs and the personal discipline involved in setting a regular time for it.

In summary, fellowship in the body results in joy.

Christ came to give believers full joy (John 16:24). This kind of joy results from pure fellowship with God and with one another. This kind of fellowship in the body is possible; God planned it that way. It is each Christian's responsibility to make fellowship in the body all that God intends it to be.

Chapter Ten

THE WITNESS OF THE BODY

The principle on which the body operates is—as we have seen—humility. The mark which distinguishes the body is love. The service of the body is to minister spiritual gifts. The fellowship of the body is sharing our love. And the purpose for which God created the body is to be a channel through which He can accomplish His will—the redemption of His people. More exactly defined, then, the body is ultimately to be edified in order that it might witness to the world.

From the beginning God has desired communication with man, endeavoring to manifest His truth to man. The crown of that revelation was the act of sending Jesus Christ into the world. In Christ, God planted His own person into a human body; but that body rose from the dead and ascended into heaven. It is no longer visible on earth.

But God, through Christ, sent the Holy Spirit to manifest Himself in another body—the body of Christ, the church. This time it was not one body physically, but many bodies, making up one spiritual body. In the church, Christ continues to dwell, through the indwelling Spirit. Christ is in the body, manifesting His glory and all His attributes, just as He did in His human body when He was here for thirty-three years. When Christ's physical body was here, He manifested love, holiness, wisdom, power, and all the glory of God. In this new body, the church, He wants to manifest the very same things: love, holiness, wisdom, power, and all the glory of God. Christians, as the body of Christ, are to manifest Christ.

God's will for this earthly body called the church, is, as Paul says in Ephesians 4:13, that all its members

> come in the unity of the faith, and of the knowledge of the Son of God . . . unto the measure of the stature of the fulness of Christ.

Christians are actually to become one body like Christ. Paul tells us God has predestinated believers to be conformed to the image of His Son (Rom. 8:28, 29). Grasp the miraculous nature of such a thing, that Christ can take our human bodies, subject to sin and death, physically frail, and make them into His temple—literally dwelling in them, planting in them His glory, that they might manifest Him to the world. What a miracle! What a demonstration of God's power in love.

Here is the key. Through this body, this collective unity of all believers, Christ wants to manifest the mighty victorious power of His person. As a body believers are to manifest Christ to the world; they are a body for witness. They are called together to be mature and edified, taught and built up that they might witness to the world. The body has diverse gifts for its edification and maturity. The more believers use these diverse gifts, the more obvious unity will become. The more we minister to each other with our gifts, the more we become one, and the more the world can see our oneness. When the world sees Christian oneness, people will know that Christ came from God.

This does not mean an individual member is excused from being a witness. People have said to me, "I don't think the Lord has called me to be a witness." That isn't so; every Christian is a witness. Every member of the body is to witness. "Ye shall receive power," said Jesus, "after that the Holy Ghost is come upon you: and ye shall be witnesses unto me." There is no option there—none at all. The Apostle Paul carefully points this out in II Corinthians 5:17, 18:

> Therefore if any man be in Christ, he is a new creature; old things are passed away; behold, all things are become new. And all things are of God, who hath reconciled us to himself by Jesus Christ, and hath given to us the ministry of reconciliation.

No Christian is excused from that. Anyone reconciled to Christ has the ministry of communicating reconciliation to others. In verse 20 of the same chapter, Paul shows us this: "Now then we are ambassadors for Christ, as though God did beseech you by us: we beg you in Christ's stead, be ye reconciled to God." Christians need to be sensitive to the truth of the New Testament about the nature of witness—as members and as a total body.

A key text dealing with this is John 15:26, 27:

> But when the Comforter is come, whom I will send unto you from the Father, even the Spirit of truth, which proceedeth from the Father, he shall testify of me: And ye also shall bear witness, because ye have been with me from the beginning.

In those two verses we discover the basic concept of the body's witness. The word "witness" is interesting, in that it takes us into a law court. We see a judge on the bench and a prisoner on trial. We hear the case argued by lawyers—first the prosecution, then the defense. Both call witnesses to substantiate their cases. The setting implies that Christians, as individual members of the body, are individual witnesses in a trial, so to speak. Who is on trial? Jesus Christ. Who is the judge? The world. Who is the defense attorney? The Holy Spirit. Who is the prosecutor? Satan with his lies and accusations. Christians are the witnesses, both as individual members and as a total body.

As individuals, believers are separate witnesses in a situation where Jesus Christ is on trial before the world. Not before the Sanhedrin, not before Pilate, and not before Herod Antipas, Jesus is on trial now at the bar of world opinion. The world judges Christ on the basis of the witnesses. Some people judge Him to be a fake; some judge Him to be a good man; others judge Him to be a teacher; others, a liar, and so on. If a witness tears down the claims of Jesus Christ by the kind of life he lives, it would be better if he were out of the courtroom altogether. He only confuses the issue. Notice the phrase used in John 15:26, "when the Comforter is come." The word "comforter" is *paracletos,* "one called alongside to help, the counsel for defense." The Holy Spirit is the Paraclete; He defends Christ. He calls members of the body to witness and confirm the testimony of Christ. All Christians are witnesses, either helping or hindering the cause of Christ.

The body witnesses by its unity (John 13:34, 35; 17:7). Can you imagine the devastating impact that a united church would have on this world? I don't mean an ecumenical church where everybody kisses doctrine good-by, throws their arms around each other, and marches off to battle over the latest social issue. The body of Christ comprising truly saved people needs to be one and, sadly, it is not. Today the body's testimony in that regard is pathetically weak. Our testimony is strife, division, carnality, and confusion. The world, then, renders its verdict on the strength of these two kinds of witnesses: the individual members of the body, and the body as a whole.

We will examine in this chapter six aspects of the

body's witness: (1) Christian witness is to the world; (2) is of the Son; (3) is by the Father; (4) is through the Holy Spirit; (5) is in the individual member; (6) is in the total body.

1. *Christian witness is to the world.* Christians will not understand the nature of their witness until they understand what the world is. In John 15 Jesus talks about its characteristics. Generated and controlled by Satan, "the world" is the entire system of evil which operates on the earth through demons and men who don't know God (cf. John 8:44). The prince and ruler of this world is the devil—the whole world is in his power. True, according to I John 2:17, the world is passing away, but while it lasts, it is the absolute antagonist of the church. The world hates the church; its hatred is deep and bitter.

The verses about the body's witness are in a context of the world's hostility and hatred.

> If the world hate you, ye know that it hated me before it hated you. If ye were of the world, the world would love his own: but because ye are not of the world, but I have chosen you out of the world, therefore the world hateth you. . . . But all these things will they do unto you for my name's sake, because they know not him that sent me. . . . If I had not done among them the works which none other man did, they had not had sin: but now have they both seen and hated both me and my Father. But this cometh to pass, that the word might be fulfilled that is written in their law, They hated me without a cause. . . . These things have I spoken unto you, that ye should not be offended. They shall put you out of the synagogues: yea, the time cometh, that whosoever killeth you will think that he doeth God service. And these things will they do unto you, because they have not known the Father, nor me (John 15:18, 19, 21, 24, 25; 16:1-3).

This whole passage is a text about the hatred of the world. In the middle of it, verses 26 and 27 clearly tell that Christian testimony and witness are to the world. The world hates, the world ostracizes, the world kills; that is the antagonism of the world. But Jesus goes on to say that believers must witness to the world. Note the first word, "But!" (v. 26). Even though the world hates, though it ostracizes, even though it kills, "But when the Comforter is come," you will confront the world and witness to it.

How is a body member to react when he is faced with the opposition of the world? If they throw him out, if he is cursed, what is he supposed to do? Retaliate in anger? No! Lick his wounds in self-pity? No! Withdraw and go back to Bible study? No! He is supposed to bear witness before the world whatever the cost—and count it all joy—to suffer in Jesus Christ's place (Col. 1:24) and that others might be saved (Phil. 1:12).

2. *Christian witness is of the Son.* "And ye also shall bear witness, because ye have been with me" (John 15:27). Testimony is to the Son. The world's hatred focuses on Jesus Christ. "They hated me without a cause" (v. 25). Christ is on trial, and Christian testimony must be of Him.

Preaching centers on Jesus Christ throughout the New Testament. John illustrates this in Revelation 1:2: "Who bare record [bore witness] of the word of God, and of the testimony of Jesus Christ." John's testimony was Christ. In Revelation 12:17, he reiterates the idea: "And the dragon was wroth with the woman, and went to make war with the remnant of her seed, which keep the commandments of God, and have the testimony of Jesus Christ." Testimony was always directly associated with Jesus Christ. In fact, John even says in Revelation 19:10b that the Old Testament witnessed to Christ: "For the testimony of Jesus is the spirit of prophecy." Christ's testimony is the character of the Old Testament prophecy.

The apostles had no doubts about this. Jesus told them before and after His death and resurrection that they were to testify of Him. In Acts 1:8 He says, "Ye shall be witnesses unto me." They obeyed. Their sermons in the early church were always about Jesus Christ. In Acts 10:38-40, Peter preached to Cornelius and said,

> God anointed Jesus of Nazareth with the Holy Ghost and with power: who went about doing good, and healing all that were oppressed of the devil; for God was with him. And we are witnesses of all things which he did both in the land of the Jews, and in Jerusalem; whom they slew and hanged on a tree: Him God raised up the third day, and shewed him openly.

Peter's sermons were always about Jesus.

Much so-called witnessing has nothing to do with Jesus Christ. It talks about religion or about the church, or vaguely about God.

We say, "I witnessed to my friend."

"What did you say?"

"Well, I kind of let him know that I go to church."

You didn't witness to your friend—that is not a witness. A witness gives testimony to Jesus Christ. Often our witnessing is an autobiography, and we never get around to Christ. We just give our spiritual life history. A Christian can give his entire "testimony," and the listener might know nothing more about Jesus than when the Christian started. Witnessing is not a discussion of your life or the church; it is a testimony to Jesus Christ! It is proclaiming the great truths of His virgin birth, sinless life, atoning death, physical resurrection, ascension, and coming again!

3. *Christian witness is by the Father.* "When the Comforter is come, whom I will send to you from the Father.... (John 15:26). When Jesus Christ sent the Spirit, He really sent God's witness to this world. For the Spirit proceeded from the Father and bore the Father's testimony. The greatest witness of Christ

is the Father; the Father is the Son's chief witness. It was the Father's supreme concern to bring honor and glory to the Son. In John 8:54, Jesus answered the Jews' question about His identity by saying, "If I honour myself, my honour is nothing; it is my Father that honoureth me." See this also:

> If I bear witness of myself, my witness is not true. There is another that beareth witness of me; and I know that the witness which he witnesseth of me is true. ... But I have greater witness than that of John: for the works which the Father hath given me to finish, the same works that I do, bear witness of me, that the Father hath sent me. And the Father himself, which hath sent me, hath borne witness of me (John 5:31, 32, 36, 37).

Jesus said, in effect, "The Father is my chief witness. He is the one primarily concerned with communicating who I am. The Spirit who proceeds from the Father is sent to carry the Father's witness and plant it within you!"

How did the Father bear witness to the Son? First, through the Old Testament. "Search the scriptures," Jesus said to the Jews, "for in them ye think ye have eternal life: and they are they which testify of me" (John 5:39). The Old Testament is all about Jesus Christ. Jesus revealed this to the disciples on the road to Emmaus: "And beginning at Moses and all the prophets, he expounded unto them in all the scriptures the things concerning himself" (Luke 24:27).

The second way in which God witnessed to His Son was through Christ's works. That is indicated in John 10:25.

> Jesus answered them, I told you, and ye believed not: the works that I do in my Father's name, they bear witness of me.

The miracles that Jesus did were the Father's witness. They showed that Jesus was who He claimed to be.

> Believest thou not that I am in the Father, and the

Father in me? the words that I speak unto you, I speak not of myself: but the Father that dwelleth in me, he doeth the works (John 14:10).

The works that Christ did were actually the works of the Father attesting to His claim to deity.

The third means of the Father's witness was by direct speaking. God actually said: "This is my beloved Son" (Matt. 17:5). The Father, then, is the source of all witness about Christ. That entire witness is recorded in Scripture: The Old Testament prophecies, the works that Jesus did, the words that He spoke, the direct statements of the Father. Christian witness should be an echo of the Father's witness. Believers should study the Word diligently, to really know the Father's witness.

4. *Christian witness is through the Spirit.*

But when the Comforter is come, whom I will send unto you from the Father, even the Spirit of truth, which proceedeth from the Father, he shall testify of me (Eph. 15:26).

Whatever witness God the Father has in the world, He has through the Holy Spirit.

The Holy Spirit has two names, "Comforter" and "Spirit of Truth." "Comforter," as we have already seen, means Paraclete and takes us into a courtroom. The Holy Spirit is Christ's defense lawyer. The Spirit calls believers into court to testify. Since He is also "the Spirit of truth," this reveals the kind of testimony He gives. He cannot be a false witness; He is truth and always declares truth. Jesus ministered in the power of the Spirit, and Christians cannot witness apart from Him.

5. *Christian witness is in the members.* Where does the Spirit dwell today? In believers. They are the vehicle carrying the witness that proceeds from the Father by the Spirit. The Holy Spirit has no physical voice, no platform to do His witnessing, except for

members of the body. When Jesus promised to send the Holy Spirit, He said, "He dwelleth with you, and shall be in you" (John 14:17). Acts 4:31 shows how the Spirit witnesses in believers: "They were all filled with the Holy Ghost, and they spake the word of God with boldness." Members of the body are individual witnesses, empowered by the resident Holy Spirit. Witnessing, then, is carrying the testimony of the Father, brought to us through the Spirit, and communicating it to the world.

Christians are qualified to witness not only because of the resident Holy Spirit, but also because they have experienced Jesus Christ firsthand. Christ's words in John 15 were directed to the disciples gathered with Him in the Upper Room, but they also apply to believers today. You can be a witness only if you experienced the thing you are testifying about. To witness in a court case you must have been personally involved; secondhand testimony is unacceptable. I will never forget when I had to go to court to testify about a crime I had seen. They asked me three things: What did you see? What did you hear? What did you feel? A witness is someone with firsthand experience—I heard it, I saw it, and I felt it. I was there. John says,

That which ... we have heard, which we have seen with our eyes, ... and our hands have handled, of the Word of life ... declare we unto you (I John 1:1, 3).

That is a witness! All you need to do is say, "I have been with Jesus Christ. I have seen Him, heard Him, and I have touched Him." Then you are a qualified witness. Body witness is not a detached lecture about Jesus; it is to say, "I want to share the Christ whom I have seen and heard and touched with my life."

Down through the ages this kind of character witness has been more precious than life itself. The word *martus,* which is the word for "witness," came to mean "martyr," because many times when believers were standing up as a witness for Christ, it cost them their lives. The body of Christ needs more men and women, more missionaries, teachers, preachers, and laymen who will witness effectively whatever the cost to their egos or their lives—witnesses who are expendable for the salvation of others.

6. *Christian witness is in the body.* The Holy Spirit indwells not only every individual member, but also the entire, collective body, the church.

> For he is our peace, who hath made both one [Jew and Gentile], and hath broken down the middle wall of partition between us; Having abolished in his flesh the enmity [that is, the antagonism between Jew and Gentile], even the law of commandments contained in ordinances; for to make in himself of twain one new man . . . For through him we both have access by one Spirit unto the Father. . . . In whom all the building fitly framed together groweth unto an holy temple in the Lord; In whom ye [plural] also are builded together for an habitation of God through the Spirit (Eph. 2:14, 15, 18, 21, 22).

The entire church, the body of Christ, is the temple of the Holy Spirit, just as the individual member is. He indwells the total body in order to carry the witness of the Father planted in the body to the world.

How can the body witness in a collective, single testimony? There are two ways. First, the body witnesses by its visible oneness. Jesus prayed,

> Neither pray I for these [disciples] alone, but for them also which shall believe on me through their word; That they all may be one; as thou Father, art in me, and I in thee, that they also may be one in us; that the world may believe that thou hast sent me (John 17:20, 21).

Today this body witness is nil because of strife, division, and confusion. We are fragmented into many small divisions, each one trying to protect its own little ideas. We haven't begun to see what God can do through a united testimony to Jesus in the church. The Spirit indwells all of us, so that our witness might be total and unified. If only the world could see us as one—what an impact!

The second way the body witnesses is by love.

Little children, yet a little while I am with you. Ye shall seek me: and as I said unto the Jews, Whither I go, ye cannot come; so now I say to you. A new commandment I give unto you, That ye love one another; as I have loved you, that ye also love one another. By this shall all men know that ye are my disciples, if ye have love one to another (John 13:33-35).

Christians would have a powerful effect on this world if they showed love for one another. O, what a witness that would be!

Individual body members are the last link in the witness of the Father. The testimony started with the Father, about the Son, through the Spirit, and came to us. Believers are the final step in the witness to Jesus Christ. The testimony of Christ must not break down at this level. Each Christian must do his part as a body member to witness individually. Each one must do his part for the body to create oneness by ministering his spiritual gift, by loving, and by fulfilling the demands of fellowship. Then the mission of the Father in sending the Son will come to pass as God intended. There is a world to be won; it will begin to be won, when we are one! And really, not until.

Epilogue

PERSONALIZING THE PRINCIPLES

The following statement is attributed to Aristides, a second century worldly philosopher. It is his comment on Christians:

> They abstain from all impurity, in the hope of the recompense that is to come in another world. As for their servants or handmaids or children, they persuade them to become Christians by the love they have for them; and when they have become so, they call them without distinction, brothers. They do not worship strange gods; and they walk in all humility and kindness and falsehood is not found among them and they love one another. When they see the stranger they bring him to their homes and rejoice over him as over a true brother; for they do not call brothers those who are after the flesh, but those who are in the Spirit and in God.
>
> And there is among them a man that is poor and needy and if they have not an abundance of necessities, they fast two or three days that they may supply the needy with the necessary food.
>
> They observe scrupulously the commandment of their Messiah; they live honestly and soberly as the Lord

their God commanded them. Every morning and all hours on account of the goodness of God toward them, they praise and laud Him and over their food and their drink, they render Him thanks.

And if any righteous person of their number passes away from this world, they rejoice and give thanks to God and they follow his body as though he were moving from one place to another. And when a child is born to them, they praise God, and if again it chances to die in its infancy, they praise God mightily, as for one who has passed through the world without sins.

Such is the law of the Christians and such is their conduct.[1]

This can be so today. It must be! God's blueprint for the body is clear. But all the plans are useless, unfulfilled, unless you and I make them part of our lives. That demands three things:

Commitment. This involves a personal vow on our part to give the totality of our lives to the priorities God has laid down for the building of Christ's body. We must be willing to be aggressively dedicated to spending ourselves to answer the prayer of our Lord for unity. We must realize we are a strategic part of a great masterpiece.

There is a famous story from the days when Sir Christopher Wren was building St. Paul's cathedral in London. Wren was making a tour one day and asked a man working on the building, "What are you doing?"

The workman replied, "I am cutting this stone to the right size."

He asked a second man working elsewhere, "What are you doing?"

"I am earning money," came the retort.

Wren came, later, to a third man and offered the

---

[1] *The Apology of Aristides,* Syriac text and translation. Cited in *Encyclopedia Britannica,* Vol. 1 (Chicago: Encyclopedia Britannica, Inc., 1929), page 346.

same query. The man paused for a second from his work and excitedly replied, "I am helping Sir Christopher Wren to build St. Paul's cathedral!"

As Christians, we must ever hold before us the loftiest ideal of our presence in the church—we are here, in the Spirit's energy, working to help the Lord Jesus Christ build His body! To this we must be committed.

Careful study. Since the principles are revealed only in the Word of God, diligent and systematic study is essential, not only for initial information and inspiration, but for repetition, that we may be constantly remembering these priorities. We must study.

Communication. These truths must be taught at all levels—pulpit, Sunday school, Bible studies, personal discipling, family devotions. The church for too long has allowed the truths to lie dormant. We must teach.

It is the most sobering thing in all this discussion to realize that the whole glorious and gracious master plan for the church in the world—with all its features designed and formed in the mind of our loving Lord and revealed to us through the marvelous process of revelation by the Spirit as the very fulfillment of His will—is finally resting for its accomplishment on us. It all comes down to whether we are faithful to commitment, careful study and communication.

Finally, brethren, farewell. Be perfect, be of good comfort, be of one mind, live in peace; and the God of love and peace shall be with you. Greet one another with an holy kiss.

All the saints salute you. The grace of the Lord Jesus Christ, and the love of God, and the communion of the Holy Ghost be with you all. Amen (II Cor. 13:11-14).